ALL THAT
SIZZLES

Easy Oriental Recipes

DAVID TSANG

House of Tsang, Inc.

ACKNOWLEDGEMENT

Any book is a team effort. I am indebted to many dedicated professionals for their hard work and enthusiasm.

To Linda Brandt, whose editorial expertise brought this whole project together and gave it the professional touch; and to Ken Coburn of Interprint, whose diligence assured quality in the production of *All That Sizzles*.

Special thanks must also go to Carrie Seeman, Jan Nix, Diane Oda, Gladys Lee, Gail Ellerbrake, Ivan Lai, and Susan Yan, for those long hours spent preparing the text and testing my recipes.

My deep gratitude to Jay Harlow, for his editorial input; to Salinda Tyson, for her marvelous artistic design; to Joanne Dexter, Steve Larson, and Larry Guyer from The Graphic Marketing Group, whose collective efforts resulted in the excellent layout and vivid photographs that grace these pages.

Finally, my thanks to Yan Can International Cooking School, whose expert guidance and professional contribution made this project such an enjoyable experience.

To my wife Cheryl, and our daughters Theresa and Marisa, for their patience and understanding; and to my partners in crime, Bill and Georgia Sher, and Steve Goldman, for their support and encouragement in all my escapades.

Table of Contents

A Word From Dave Tsang 6

Culinary Regions of China ▪ Tools For Good Cooking ▪ Slice & Dice ▪ Stir, Braise & Glaze ▪ Deep-frying & Red Cooking ▪ Steam & Flash Cooking ▪ Oriental Pantry ▪ Plan Your Own Menu ▪ Oriental Beverages

Instant Impressions 38

Recipes for Less than 15 minutes

Garden Dynasty ▪ Singapore Sins ▪ Black & White Pyramids ▪ Fiery Roots of Spring ▪ Emerald Bonsai ▪ Seasonal Harvest ▪ Szechuan Fowl Play ▪ Rice In A Rush ▪ Gold Velvet ▪ Mandarin Treasure ▪ Turkey Bundles ▪ Chicken Power ▪ Laughing Clams ▪ South China Sea Catch ▪ Fish Fillet Olé ▪ Bronze Swimmer ▪ Fowl For All Seasons ▪ Emperor's Good Fortune ▪ Belles & Beef ▪ Blue Plate Special ▪ Steak Oriental ▪ Sanjook ▪ Family Fare ▪ Mixed Media

Timely Temptations 70

Recipes for Less than 30 minutes

Golden Triangles ▪ Ming Coins ▪ Spicy Spuds ▪ Rice To The Occasion ▪ East-West Omelet ▪ Naked Noodles ▪ Szechuan Noodle Toss ▪ East-West Salad ▪ Korean Donburi ▪ Tangy Bird ▪ Flower Drums ▪ Crescent Moons ▪ Tsang Tempura ▪ Guangzhou Scallops ▪ Kung Pao Shrimp ▪ Scarlet Warrior ▪ Beijing Burgers ▪ Asian Beef ▪ Mongolian Fire Pot ▪ Pagoda Pork Chops ▪ Chinese Sausage Grill ▪ Sweet & Sour Pork ▪ Empress-style Pears ▪ Rainbow Fruit Medley

Savory Sensations 102
Recipes for Less than 1 hour

Dragon's Broth • Tsang Spring Rolls • Chinese Flap Jacks • Potstickers • Bombay Madness • Savory Chicken Wings • From The Garden • Peking Chicken Skewers • Yellow Sea Dragon • Sisters From The Sea • Seoul Bones • Time-to-spare Ribs • Mu Shu Pork • Mongolian Lamb • Toishan Veal • Tropical Ices • Make A Fortune • Asian Sesame Crisps

Classical Creations 126
Recipes for more than 1 hour

Foil-wrapped Chicken • Char Siu Bow • Indonesian Turnovers • Siu Mai • Sizzling Rice Soup • Won Ton Soup • Soto Ayam • Korean Fire & Ice • Char Siu • Cantonese Ribs • Red-cooked Lamb • Repeat Performance • Mandarin Pancakes • Imperial Peking Duck • Nesting Chicken • Golden Phoenix • Chinese Chicken in Clay • Critic's Choice • Show Stoppers • Lobster David • Catch-of-the-Day • Emperor's Secret • Heavenly Cloud • Tsang Tarts • Eight Treasures

Index 157

A Word From David Tsang
Techniques, Equipment & More

I often ask people if they "live to eat" or "eat to live." While both phrases may sound extreme, I find it's a unique way of discovering more about one's personality and in particular, just how they feel about food.

Some of us lean towards "living to eat." We heartily enjoy a variety of good food and usually prefer creating it, as well.

On the other hand, some of us are forced into that fast-paced "eat to live" syndrome. You know what that's like—a quick burger and fries eaten on the run.

I wrote <u>All That Sizzles</u> for both kinds of people because I'm convinced that, even though a lack of time forces some of us to lose interest in what we eat, good food and the preparation of it, should be an option available for us all.

Let me show you how to cook exciting, Oriental dishes in your own kitchen in just minutes.

Glance through the first chapter for a quick review about cutting and cooking techniques and types of equipment used. You'll find a friendly glossary that identifies over 45 common and unusual ingredients used in Oriental cooking.

Unlike most cookbooks, <u>All That Sizzles</u> is divided into chapters according to the length of cooking and preparation time. So if you're in a rush and have only 15 minutes to cook, select recipes in the chapter called "Instant Impressions". Other chapters contain recipes for 30 minutes, less than 1 hour and for more than 1 hour.

You probably recognize the names of some recipes—Mu Shu Pork, Potstickers, Peking Duck and, of course, Fortune Cookies. But we've added a touch of whimsy to the names of the others. Don't tell me your guests won't be curious when they find out you're serving "Singapore Sins" and "Szechuan Fowl Play" for dinner.

I truly believe it's important for all of us to "live to eat" a little bit more, rather than just "eating to live". Don't you agree?

CULINARY REGIONS OF CHINA

Q. What are the different cooking regions of China?

A. China is a large country with many climates. Regional flavors and styles of cooking are strongly influenced by climate and natural resources. There are basically 4 regional styles:

• The Southern style centers in Guangzhou (Canton) and lies at the southern tip of China. The climate is tropical and rainy, with plenty of fresh produce year round. This cooking style emphasizes fresh natural flavors. Only light seasonings are used, so as not to mask nature's best.

• The Western style includes the province of Szechuan and is located in the middle of China. The climate is hot, humid, and muggy. Most dishes include spicy hot peppers or hot chili oil to spark appetites. Pickled relishes and preserved vegetables are common.

• The Northern style is represented by Peking, once the home of the Imperial courts. Winters are cold, but in the warm season, wheat is grown. Therefore, noodles and pancakes are more popular than rice, which is grown more in the southern region. Spicy seasonings are used in Northern cooking also.

• The Eastern style, influenced by the coastal region, takes advantage of the variety of fish and seafood available. It is also known for red-cooking, and often a small addition of salt and sugar is used to enhance flavor.

TOOLS FOR GOOD COOKING

Some people think that Chinese cooking is complicated and troublesome, and that it takes years of practice to do it with ease. The truth is, Chinese cooking is no more complicated or troublesome than most of the meals you prepare at home. Most dishes can be prepared with just a few basic tools. Many of my students ask similar questions about the tools and utensils needed for Chinese cooking. The following information should clarify any questions you have.

Q. I already have a well-stocked kitchen. What else should I get for Oriental cooking?

A. A wok with accessories, a cleaver, and a steamer.

Q. What's the advantage of using a wok?

A. The curved shape of a wok produces graduated temperature zones which allow you to cook many different ingredients without having to remove them from the wok. The bottom of the wok next to the flame is very hot and can be used for searing and sealing. Push food up along the sloping side walls of the wok to keep it warm. This gives you room to stir-fry other ingredients.

Q. What is the best size wok to buy? What should it be made of?

A. I prefer a 12 or 14-inch flat-bottomed carbon steel wok. Since many households have electric burners, a flat-bottomed wok allows good heat transfer from the burner to the wok. Flat-bottomed woks also work well on gas burners. Steel is best for fast and even heat conduction, and it is durable.

Q. What is "seasoning" the wok all about?

"A wok is the single most important tool of a Chinese chef."

A. Seasoning the wok means leaving a layer of something on the wok so it won't rust or stick. However, I don't like to do this, so I always scrub my wok with hot soapy water. To prevent it from rusting, I place the wok back on the burner as soon as I wash it, over medium-high heat to dry. When cooking, I first heat the wok before adding oil, then to minimize sticking, I let the oil heat before adding the raw ingredients. Be sure to use a high temperature oil such as Wok Oil.

Q. I always associate a wok with stir-frying. Can I do anything else in the wok?

A. The wok is very versatile. You can use it for steaming, deep-frying, braising, simmering, stewing, boiling water, and cooking rice.

Q. Do I need to prepare a new wok for use?

A. Since woks are made of many different types of metals, always read the manufacturer's directions. However, there are a few steps to follow to prepare a new wok for use:

• Scrub the wok with a scouring pad in hot, soapy water to remove the protective coating applied at the factory.

• Dry the wok with a cloth and immediately place on a burner over medium-high heat for about a minute to dry completely. Now it is ready.

Q. I have an electric wok, but find my cooking times vary with the recipes. Why do stir-fried dishes take so much longer in an electric wok?

A. Most electric woks are teflon-coated and do not transfer heat very well. One of the principles of stir-

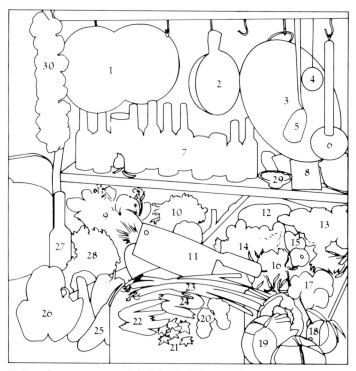

1) Bamboo steamer with lid 2) Chinese clay pot 3) Large steel wok 4) Small wire strainer 5) Stainless steel spatula 6) Wire strainer 7) House of Tsang products: Mandarin Marinade, Wok Oil, Sweet & Sour Stir Fry Sauce, Classic Stir Fry Sauce, Szechuan Spicy Stir Fry Sauce, Korean Teriyaki Sauce, Hoisin Sauce, Spicy Brown Bean Sauce, Hot Chili Sesame Oil, and Mongolian Fire Oil *(fermented black beans in carton, rear)* 8) Tsang and Ma seed packets 9) Chinese mustard greens and bok choy 10) Cilantro *(Chinese parsley)* 11) Chinese cleaver 12) Bean thread noodles 13) Dried red chili peppers *(foreground)*; fresh ginger *(rear)* 14) Dried wood ears *(foreground)*; dried lychees *(rear)* 15) Dried black mushrooms 16) Dried tiger lily buds 17) Fresh water chestnuts 18) Tangerine 19) Shanghai hairy crab 20) Dried lychees *(foreground);* dried black mushrooms *(rear)* 21) Star anise 22) Snow peas 23) Green onions 24) Raw shrimp 25) Oriental eggplants 26) Red and green bell peppers 27) House of Tsang Dark Soy Sauce 28) Chinese *(napa)* cabbage 29) Szechuan peppercorns 30) Garlic braid.

FLAVORS OF THE ORIENT

"A good, sharp cleaver is worth a thousand knives."

frying is to cook food at a high heat to sear in juices and nutrients. Try cooking just 2 cups of ingredients at a time. This might help.

Q. What other tools are useful?

A. A wok stand, to provide a secure base for the round-bottomed wok while steaming and deep-frying; a wok cover (a high domed lid) used for steaming; a ladle and Chinese spatula, whose design angle follows the contour of the wok; a wire strainer, (mesh skimmer), available in various sizes with long handles, and used for deep-frying, skimming, or re-moving vegetables and noodles from hot water; bamboo or wood cooking chopsticks, about 14 inches long, used like tongs to turn deep-fried foods, toss food while stir-frying, or mix ingredients.

Q. Do I need a Chinese cleaver?

A. No need to panic if you do not have a Chinese cleaver, just use a regular chef's knife. However, a cleaver can be used to slice vegetables, mince, chop, and tenderize meat, and with the wide blade you can scoop cut-up food from a cutting board. My mother always uses the handle to crush garlic and black beans. Cleavers come in several weights. Choose one that feels comfortable in your hand. After a few tries at slicing and dicing, you'll feel at home with this seemingly intimidating, but functional tool.

Q. What types of steamers are available?

A. You can buy stackable sets of bamboo steamers so 2 or 3 different dishes can be steamed at the same time when set in a wok filled with water. The steam-ers come in several different sizes; a steamer with a 12-inch diameter is a good size for a 14-inch wok.

Metal steamers are quite good and are self-contained units - an advantage if you want to steam and stir-fry simultaneously. When using a metal steamer, place a clean dish towel under the cover to absorb the water that collects under the lid. This is especially important when steaming buns, dumplings, or other foods which would become soggy from condensation.

SLICE & DICE

Did you ever notice that Oriental food is usually served in bite-size pieces? Small pieces of food cook faster, thus allowing flavor and nutrients to be seared and sealed inside. Small pieces are also convenient to eat — no cutting utensils are needed at the table. Review the cutting techniques on the following pages. Each has a special use in Oriental cooking.

Q. What is the difference between the cutting I normally do and the Chinese cutting techniques?

A. There is very little difference except for roll-cutting or slicing on the diagonal. The reason Chinese cut food in different ways is to optimize the texture, flavor, and cooking time. Here are the different Chinese cutting techniques:

• Slicing - Most common cutting technique. With a sharp cleaver (or chef's knife), cut straight down through the meat or vegetable into slices of the required thickness. Vegetables like carrots are thinly sliced on the diagonal (or slant) to expose more surface area for even cooking.

• Chopping - Cutting through large bones (like cutting spareribs in thirds, or splitting a chicken in eighths). A heavy–duty chopping cleaver is the best tool to use. Use one hard, straight downward motion.

CUTTING TECHNIQUES

◀ *Slicing eggplant*

Julienne strips ▶
of red pepper

◀ *Dicing zucchini*

Shredding ▶
cabbage

◀ *Mincing red*
pepper

Roll-cutting ▶
carrot

"Crushing garlic with the broad side of a cleaver helps to release more flavor."

Do not chop bones with the standard medium-weight cleaver.

• Mincing - Minced food is cut into fine, irregular pieces, much smaller than diced. Guide the cleaver, or chef's knife, in an up and down, side to side motion, cutting all the ingredients into little pieces.

• Crushing - Used for garlic and ginger. Place food on a cutting board and hit sharply with the broad side of the cleaver (keep sharp edge away from yourself). This is a good way to remove skin from a clove of garlic before mincing. Crushing helps to release more flavor from garlic and ginger when they are cooked.

• Dicing & Cubing - Diced food is uniformly cut into ¼-inch squares. Cubed food is slightly larger and usually measures ½-inch square. If the ingredient is irregularly shaped, triangles or other shapes can be cut to conform to the approximate size.

• Matchstick - Also called julienne. Cut food into ⅛ to ¼- inch thick slices, 2 inches long. Stack a few pieces at a time and cut vertically through the stack into pieces the size of wooden matchsticks.

• Roll Cutting - Used to cut cylindrical foods like zucchini and carrots. Trim and discard root ends of vegetable. Start at either end and slice at a 45-degree angle. Roll the food a quarter turn, and slice again at the same angle. Continue cutting and turning until done. This technique makes pieces about the same size, but with a greater cooking surface area.

• Shredding - Also called cutting into slivers. First, cut the food into fairly thin slices. Then stack the slices, a few at a time, and cut vertically into the stack to produce fine threadlike shreds, about 2 to 3 inches long.

"When you stir-fry, listen for the sizzle, smell the aroma, and watch the colors and flavors harmonize."

STIR, BRAISE & GLAZE

Oriental cooking is more than just stir-frying. Different cooking methods are used to bring out the best flavor and texture of all the ingredients. Which techniques do what... read on and find out.

Q. What are the most common cooking techniques used to prepare Chinese food?

A. Stir-frying is the most popular, and steaming runs a close second. Many people believe all Chinese dishes are deep-fried, but this is not true - this technique is mainly used for appetizers. Red-cooking is a term unfamiliar to Westerners. It is the technique of slow cooking with a sauce, similar to braising. In China, roasting (but, not in the oven) is more like barbecuing.

Q. What are the secrets of stir-frying?

A. Stir-frying is a technique that needs extremely high heat. Heat is used to seal in juices and flavors of all the ingredients. Listed below are hints to guarantee successful stir-frying:

• Have everything ready before you start to cook.

• Cut and slice all the ingredients into similar shapes and uniform sizes to ensure fast, even cooking.

• Group vegetables with similar cooking times together in bowls.

• Preheat the wok over high heat for 1 to 2 minutes. Add the oil and swirl it around in the wok. When the oil ripples (just before it begins to smoke), add fresh garlic, ginger, and onion slices to flavor the oil. The Chinese call this process of flavoring the oil "hei wok". As an alternative, use House of Tsang Wok Oil, a high temperature cooking oil seasoned with garlic, onion, and ginger.

• Use an oil with a high smoking point, which enables it to withstand high temperatures without burning. The most common home cooking oil for stir-frying is peanut oil. Restaurants use cottonseed oil. However, safflower, soybean, or corn oil are good, too. Butter, margarine, and olive oil are not suitable for stir-frying.

• Stir-fry the meat first, just until it changes color, then remove it from the wok. Cook vegetables next, adding the firm vegetables first. Always maintain a high heat level. Listen for the "sizzling" sound - if it stops, the wok is not hot enough. Be careful not to add too much food to the wok at one time, or the heat level will drop.

• When you stir-fry, listen for the sizzle and smell the aroma.

• To complete the dish, return the meat to the wok and add sauce if you wish. Add some very dry sherry and a few drops of Pure Sesame Seed Oil at the end to perk up flavor and aroma.

• Serve stir-fried dishes immediately for the best flavor and aroma. If you have to keep them warm for awhile, slightly undercook the vegetables.

DEEP-FRYING AND RED-COOKING

Q. Are most Chinese dishes deep-fried?

A. No. Many people enjoy deep-fried food and order egg rolls and sweet and sour pork in restaurants because deep-frying makes food crispy, colorful, and

"The secret is to fry fast and at just the right temperature."

tasty. But Chinese very seldom prepare deep-fried dishes for their own everyday meals.

Q. Any secrets for making crispy, deep-fried food?

A. The secret is to fry fast, at the proper temperature, and serve the food hot. Do not put food into oil until the oil is hot enough, normally around 360° to 375°F., and don't add too much food at one time. Overloading the pan lowers the temperature of the oil and causes the food to become greasy and sodden. Use a deep-frying thermometer - it's the easiest way to be certain you are maintaining a constant oil temperature.

Q. Can I reuse deep-fry oil?

A. Yes. If you've cooked fish, then save that oil only for cooking seafood. Filter, by pouring cool oil through a fine strainer or cheesecloth, and funnel into a clean jar. Cover and refrigerate oil until needed; discard it when it darkens or begins to smell rancid.

Q. What is red-cooking?

A. Red-cooking is the Chinese technique of braising food in a mixture of broth, soy sauce, and seasonings; star anise is one of the favorite spices to use. Food can be initially browned to seal in the juices and then covered with liquid. When cooked, food becomes reddish-brown in color, hence its name. Beef, pork, and lamb can be red-cooked very well.

STEAMING & FLASH COOKING

Q. Are steamed dishes popular?

A. Very much so. Food that is steamed preserves the most natural flavor and nutrition. Foods are more tender and juicy, and less greasy because no additional oil is needed. The stackable, tiered steamers enable many dishes to be steamed at the same time, saving fuel and time.

Q. How do you steam?

A. Whether using multiple-tiered Chinese bamboo steamers, a stacked metal steamer, or just a regular rack placed in a wok, the food, or the dish containing the food, should be at least 1 inch above boiling water. Start with a container full of steam and keep it that way. Begin with enough water to last the full cooking time; if you need to add more, make sure it's boiling when you pour it in. Though steam looks harmless, it can burn you. Always lift the steamer lid away from you.

Q. What is "flash cooking"?

A. This literally means cooking in a flash. Food is quickly placed in a pot of rapidly boiling water and then removed, very similar to water blanching or parboiling. This technique is extremely useful for vegetables with heavy stalks, like broccoli and cauliflower, and green beans. To flash cook, heat water in a large pot. When the water boils, add a small amount of cut vegetables and cook for a few seconds, then immediately remove vegetables with a skimmer or slotted spoon. The vegetables will continue to cook a bit because of the heat. To stop the cooking, rinse the vegetables in cold water.

ORIENTAL PANTRY

Baby Corn

These tender ears of miniature corn have a mild, sweet flavor and give a wonderful texture to soups, salads, and stir-fried dishes. They are available canned (for cooking), and pickled (as an appetizer). Rinse canned baby corn before using.

Storage: In a covered container, submerged in water, refrigerate. Change water daily.
(Up to 1 week)

Bamboo Shoots

These edible shoots of the bamboo plant introduce a crunchy texture and a mild, sweet flavor to many Oriental dishes . They are sold in cans, either whole or sliced. Rinse shoots before cooking.

Storage: In a covered container, submerged in water, refrigerate.
Change water daily. (Up to 10 days)

Cabbage,
Chinese (Napa)

This compact head with pale green, oblong leaves resembles romaine lettuce. Its zestiness and crispness go well with stir-fried and braised dishes. It is also excellent pickled. Available year round.

Storage: In a plastic bag (unwashed), refrigerate.
(Up to 5 days)

Chili Oil

House of Tsang offers two fiery oils: Hot Chili Sesame Oil * (a blend of classic pure sesame seed oil and hot chili peppers) and Mongolian Fire Oil * (a hot, spicy oil with a touch of ginger, garlic, and onion). Both oils can be used as a flavoring or table condiment to add a touch of hotness to any dish.

Storage: After opening, store in a cool, dry place.
(Up to 6 months)

Cilantro

Also called Chinese parsley or fresh coriander. It

resembles Western parsley but has a much stronger flavor. Cilantro leaves (chopped) give a zesty taste to soups, poultry, or other dishes. Use whole sprigs of cilantro as a garnish.

Storage: Rinse under cold running water, shake off excess moisture, wrap in paper towel, refrigerate in a plastic bag.
(Up to 5 days)

Classic Stir Fry Sauce *

This Cantonese-style House of Tsang sauce is made from soy sauce, ginger, garlic, wine, and spices. Use it to flavor stir-fried meat, poultry, seafood, and vegetables; as a marinade or as a table condiment.

Storage: After opening, refrigerate.
(Up to 6 months)

Cornstarch

Use in marinades to seal in the natural juices of meats, to dry–coat meat for deep-frying, and to thicken sauces. When used for thickening, mix 1 part constarch with 2 parts water. Stir well before using since cornstarch tends to settle at the bottom.

Curry

A combination of turmeric, coriander, cloves, cardamom, ginger, mace, peppers, and other spices. It is available in powder, paste, or oil form.
The House of Tsang Singapore Curry Oil *
infuses these spices with oil. Use it when you desire curry flavor in stir-fried dishes, marinades, or dressings.

Storage: After opening, store Singapore Curry Oil * in a cool, dry place.
(Up to 6 months)

Daikon

Also called Japanese or Oriental radish, daikon resembles a large, white carrot. It is crisp, juicy, mildly pungent, and tastes a bit hotter than an ordinary radish. Use it in soups, stir-fried, braised, or in casserole dishes.

Storage: In a plastic bag (unwashed), refrigerate. (Up to 2 weeks)

Eggplant, Chinese

A pale purple, slender vegetable with few seeds and a thin tender skin. It has a sweeter and more delicate flavor than regular globe-shaped eggplant and can be steamed, stir–fried, deep-fried, or stuffed with ground meat or shrimp or fish paste. When Chinese eggplant is not available, use regular eggplant.

Storage: In a plastic bag (unwashed), refrigerate. (Up to 5 days)

Five-Spice, Chinese

A traditional, aromatic spice mix composed of star anise, cloves, cinnamon, fennel, and Szechuan peppercorns. Use it (sparingly) in marinades for meat and poultry, in braised dishes, casseroles, and on barbecued or roasted meat. Chinese five-spice comes in bottles or plastic packages.

Storage: In an air-tight container, in a cool, dry place. (Up to 6 months)

Ginger, Candied

Sweet, pungent condiment packed in syrup in porcelain jars, or candied and sold packaged. Serve it as a candy, or add to desserts when ginger flavor is desired.

Storage: In original container, in a cool, dry place. (Up to 3 months)

Ginger, Fresh

Fresh ginger is indispensable in Oriental cooking. The knobby, beige root (actually a rhizome or underground stem) tastes spicy and pungent when mature. Younger ginger, recognizable by its thin pink–tinged skin, is milder and more aromatic.

Storage: Mature ginger - in a cool, dry place (up to 2 weeks). Young ginger - refrigerate (up to 2 weeks).

For longer storage, peel and thinly slice ginger, store

in a jar, covered with dry sherry, refrigerate. (up to 6 months)

Hoisin Sauce *	Literally translated from Chinese to mean "sauce from fresh seafood", it is made from fermented soybeans, vinegar, garlic, sugar, and other spices. Hoisin sauce is thick and brown, with a delicious spicy-sweet taste that compliments barbecued or stir-fried dishes. House of Tsang Hoisin Sauce * can be used as a seasoning or as a condiment in classic dishes such as Mu Shu Pork and Peking Duck.

Storage: After opening, refrigerate. (Up to 6 months) |
| **Hot Mustard, Chinese** | Similar to regular mustard, but much hotter, it is used as a table condiment as well as in a dipping sauce for meat, seafood, or dumplings. It comes in powder or pre-mixed paste form. To make mustard paste, add water to the powder and stir to desired consistency.

Storage: Powder - in an air-tight container, in a cool, dry place. (Up to 12 months) Paste - in a screw-top jar, refrigerate. (Up to 6 months) |
| **Korean Teriyaki Sauce *** | This unique House of Tsang sauce is sweet, with a pleasant spicy flavor. The sesame seed and onion flavors that are added to the soy-wine base make it ideal for stir-frying, braising, or as a basting sauce for barbecued seafood, meat, and poultry. It is also delicious as a table condiment.

Storage: After opening, refrigerate. (Up to 6 months) |
| **Lychee** | Sweet, succulent walnut-size fruit from Southeast Asia. Available fresh in Chinese markets when in season during July and August, or canned in light syrup, or dried to resemble raisins. With fresh ly- |

chees, peel off the rough red skin to reach the white juicy pulp. Use lychees to enhance sweet and sour dishes or simply as a dessert.

Storage: Canned - keep unused portion in original syrup, refrigerate.
(Up to 5 days)

Mandarin Marinade *

The House of Tsang Mandarin Marinade * is a vintage marinade blending soy sauce, wine, spices, and traditional Chinese herbs. Use it to marinate and flavor meats, poultry, or fish.

Storage: After opening, refrigerate. (Up to 6 months)

Mushrooms, Dried Black

Richly-flavored, aromatic mushrooms that combine well with most ingredients. They are prized for both flavor and texture. Soak in warm water for 30 minutes to soften before cooking. Always remove hard stems.

Storage: In a plastic bag, in a cool, dry place.
(Up to 6 months)

Mushrooms, Straw

Another name for them is "umbrella mushrooms". They are dark brown, with bulb-like caps and a slightly crunchy texture and a mild flavor. Available canned, straw mushrooms give soup and stir-fried dishes a tender smooth texture. Rinse them before using.

Storage: In a covered container, submerged in water, refrigerate.
Change water daily.
(Up to 1 week)

Noodles, Bean Thread

Also called cellophane noodles, shining noodles, or transparent noodles. They are made from mung bean flour and are packed in tight bundles. Soak them in water to soften before cooking. Use bean threads in soups, stir-fried dishes, or casseroles. Their neutral flavor absorbs the taste of other foods. When deep-fried, bean threads puff up and become crisp. (Do not soak noodles before deep–frying.)

Storage: In an air-tight bag, in a cool, dry place. (Up to 6 months)

Noodles, Chinese	Made from wheat flour, often containing egg, these noodles are called "mein" in Chinese. They are sold in various thicknesses, fresh or dried. Cook noodles in a large pot of boiling water until tender but firm to the bite before using.

Storage: Fresh noodles - in a plastic bag, refrigerate (up to 5 days) or freeze (up to 3 months).

Dried noodles - in an air-tight bag, in a cool, dry place (up to 6 months).

Noodles, Rice Stick	Made from rice flour, these noodles are called "mai fun". They are thin and more brittle than bean thread noodles. Deep-fry rice stick noodles to use as a garnish, in salads, or in other dishes, or soak them in warm water to soften, then use in soups, stir-fried dishes, and casseroles.

Storage: In an air-tight bag, in a cool, dry place. (Up to 6 months)

Oyster Sauce	A rich, dark brown sauce made from oyster extract, sugar, salt, and cornstarch. It is available in bottles of various sizes. Oyster sauce is very popular in Cantonese cooking and gives a flavor boost to meat, poultry, seafood, and vegetable dishes. It is also used as a table condiment and as a dipping sauce.

Storage: After opening, refrigerate. (Up to 3 months)

Plum Sauce	Made from salted yellow plums, sweet potato, vine-

gar, sugar, and spices, it has a sweet, tangy, and pungent taste. Plum sauce is particularly popular to serve with duck, or as a dipping sauce for appetizers such as egg rolls. Use it also as a seasoning in sweet and sour dishes. Plum sauce is available in cans or bottles.

Storage: Transfer unused portion to an air-tight jar, refrigerate.
(Up to 6 months)

Preserved Vegetables, Szechuan

Pickled mustard green seasoned with salt, chili powder, and Szechuan peppercorns. It is hot, spicy, and pungent and comes in cans or plastic bags. Thinly slice to use as a flavoring ingredient with meat, poultry, and seafood dishes.

Storage: In an air-tight container, refrigerate.
(Up to 6 months)

Rice, Long–Grain

The main staple in Asia, long–grain rice is the favored rice in Chinese cooking. Fluffy and dry when cooked, it is the ideal partner to all Chinese dishes.

Storage: Raw rice - In a covered jar or container, in a cool, dry place.
(Up to 6 months)

Steamed rice - In a covered container, refrigerate.
(Up to 3 days)

Cooked rice can be re-steamed or used in fried rice.

Rice, Medium–Grain

Medium-grain rice is more moist and more sticky than the long–grain variety and is commonly used in Japanese and Korean cooking.

Storage: See long–grain.

Rice, Short–Grain

Short–grain or glutinous rice is flavorful and much more sticky when cooked. It is used mainly in preparing desserts (as a dough for wrapping) or in combination with other ingredients to make a filling for Chinese tamales (wrapped in lotus leaves).

Storage: See long–grain.

Sausage, Chinese

Called "lop cheong" in Chinese, these slightly sweet and flavorful dried seasoned links are made from spiced lean and fat pork. One variety also contains pork or duck liver.

 Cook all sausages before serving. Add thin slices to stir-fried dishes for extra flavoring. Steam or simmer whole sausages for 15 minutes, then slice and serve as a side dish.

Storage: In a plastic bag, refrigerate (up to 1 month) or freeze (Up to 6 months).

Sesame Oil

House of Tsang's Pure Sesame Seed Oil * is a concentrated, brown, aromatic oil made from roasted sesame seeds. It comes in bottles and is used as a seasoning in marinades and in soups, or to give a flavor boost to a variety of dishes before serving. House of Tsang's Hot Chili Sesame Oil* is a blend of flavorful sesame oil with a touch of hotness. It gives a distinctive Oriental character to any dish.

Storage: After opening, store bottle in a cool, dry place.(Up to 6 months)

Soy Sauce

Soy sauce is the most frequently used seasoning sauce in Oriental dishes. It is made from soybeans, wheat, salt, and water and comes in bottles of various sizes. The House of Tsang Dark Soy Sauce * gives a rich color and full-bodied flavor and is ideal for all dishes. The House of Tsang Ginger Flavored Soy Sauce * blends in clear, crisp ginger aroma and flavor. Both soy sauces can be used in marinades and stir-fried and all other dishes.

Storage: After opening, store bottle in a cool, dry place.(Up to 6 months)

Spicy Brown Bean Sauce*

This House of Tsang sauce is made from naturally fermented soy beans blended with traditional spices and herbs. Use in any recipe which calls for soy sauce or yellow bean sauce. This uniquely seasoned sauce is also perfect for steaming fish.

Storage: After opening, refrigerate.
(Up to 6 months)

Star Anise

This star-shaped, licorice-flavored spice is commonly used as a flavor enhancer in braised, stewed, or barbecued dishes. Note: Discard star anise before serving.

Storage: In an airtight container, in a cool, dry place.
(Up to 6 months)

Sweet Red Bean Paste

A smooth, sweet paste made from red beans and sugar. It is used as a filling in wheat or rice flour buns and in a variety of pastries and sweet desserts.

Storage: Transfer unused portion to an air-tight container, refrigerate.
(Up to 1 month)

Sweet & Sour Stir Fry Sauce *

This House of Tsang sauce is a blend of rice vinegar, sugar, tomato paste, and Oriental spices. Pleasant and tangy, with a hint of sweetness, it is perfect for any sweet and sour dish, and a complete condiment for all your cooking.

Storage: After opening, refrigerate.
(Up to 6 months)

Szechuan Peppercorns

These reddish-brown peppercorns have a mildly hot flavor and a pleasantly pungent aroma. For optimum flavor, lightly toast peppercorns over low heat until fragrant, then coarsely grind before using.

Storage: In an air-tight container, in a cool, dry place.
(Up to 6 months)

Szechuan Spicy Stir Fry Sauce*	House of Tsang has created this zesty hot and spicy sauce from traditional Szechuan and Hunan spices. It is tangy but with a hint of sweetness and is perfect to season all meat, poultry, seafood, or vegetable dishes. As with many other House of Tsang sauces, Szechuan Spicy Stir Fry Sauce* will also make a great table condiment.

Storage: After opening, refrigerate.
(Up to 6 months)

Tiger Lily Buds	Also called "golden needles". They are normally about 3 inches in length and resemble dry, brown noodles. The taste is delicate, musky, and slightly sweet. Tiger lily buds are used both to give flavor and to take flavor from other ingredients. Soak them in water for 30 minutes before using. Cut off and discard hard tips.

Storage: In an airtight container, in a cool, dry place.
(Up to 6 months)

Tofu	Soy bean curd, or "doufu" in Chinese, is made from soybeans and is high in calcium and protein. It has a smooth texture and a bland flavor, making it ideal to take on other flavors in a dish. There are 3 kinds of tofu available in the market: soft (smooth silky texture for soup); regular (Japanese-style bean curd); and firm (Chinese-style bean curd). Regular tofu is slightly softer and more delicately flavored than firm bean curd, but you can use the two interchangeably as an ingredient in salads, dips, soups, and stir-fried and braised dishes.

Deep-fried or pressed bean curds (for salads and other dishes) are available in Oriental stores.

Storage: In a covered container, submerged in water, refrigerate.
Change water daily.
(Up to 5 days)

Vinegar, Rice	Three kinds of rice vinegar are commonly used in Chinese cooking — white, red, and black. White is used for sweet and sour dishes; red for dipping sauces; and black is mostly used as a table condiment or for braising. Regular distilled white vinegar or red wine vinegar may be substituted for rice vinegar.

Storage: After opening, store in a cool, dry place. (Up to 6 months) |
| Water Chestnuts | Crunchy, white tuber with a sweet taste. Water chestnuts are available fresh when in season, or in cans, whole or sliced. Peel off brownish-black skin on fresh water chestnuts. Rinse canned water chestnuts before using.

Storage: In a covered container, submerged in water, refrigerate. Change water daily. (Up to 1 week) |
| Wine, Rice | Chinese rice wine is generally 60 to 80 proof. Shao Hsing wine (40 proof) is widely used in Northern Chinese cooking. Dry sherry is a good substitute.

Storage: After opening, store in a cool, dry place. (Up to 6 months) |
| Wok Oil * | The House of Tsang has created this famous Wok Oil * which blends garlic, ginger, onion, and other natural spices with oil. Use it in stir-fried dishes, in marinades, or as an all-purpose cooking oil. Its balanced flavor and aroma give all your dishes instant character.

Storage: After opening, store in a cool, dry place. (Up to 6 months) |
| Wood Ears | Also referred to as tree mushrooms. These fungi are prized for their unique crunchy texture. Bland in flavor, they readily absorb flavors from other foods and give a contrast in color. Wood ears are thicker- |

walled than cloud ears, a similar but smaller fungi. Soak them in warm water for 30 minutes to soften before cooking.

Storage: In an air-tight container, in a cool, dry place. (Up to 6 months)

Wrappers

Wheat flour wrappers for Chinese pastries come in many forms. Won ton wrappers, 3-inch squares of pastry, are used to wrap up a savory filling before boiling for soup or deep-frying for an appetizer. Gyoza wrappers are cut into circles and used to make pot stickers. If you cannot find gyoza wrappers, trim wonton wrappers to make circles. Egg roll wrappers measure about 6-inches square. Similar in size to egg roll wrappers but thinner, spring roll wrappers give a crisper and more delicate crust after frying. Look for all types of wrappers in Oriental markets.

When working with wrappers, avoid prolonged exposure to air - they tend to dry out quickly if not covered.

Storage: In plastic wrap, refrigerate (up to 1 week) or freeze (up to 3 months).

* House of Tsang Product

PLAN YOUR OWN MENU

The secret for managing your time in the kitchen is more than quick and easy recipes. There are other things to consider, like the proper way of slicing vegetables (for rapid heat penetration), marinating meat and poultry, pre-mixing the seasoning sauce, and saving leftovers. Even shopping for the right cut of meat can be an important consideration to achieve kitchen efficiency.

Read through my suggestions, and you will save yourself time, energy, and aggravation. Remember, a minute saved at the stove is a minute savored at the table.

Food is the ideal "sharing" experience. I can't think of a better way to enjoy your family and friends than to share a delightful meal with them. Planning a dinner party at home or in a restaurant doesn't have to be an impossible task. Let me share some of my personal experiences in "engineering" fun and memorable dinners.

Q. What are the ways to save time when cooking Oriental food?

A. You can make a delicious and nutritious Oriental dish in just 15 to 30 minutes, if you economize on time and motion. Let's take an example of a simple stir-fried dish, since the actual cooking time is normally less than 5 minutes. Here are some tips to shorten preparation time:

• BE PREPARED! Plan ahead and design a menu you can manage. Read through each recipe before starting to cook.

"Look for a balance of flavors, textures, and colors for each dish."

• When you are short of time, purchase ingredients that will save you time. Get boneless cuts of meat or ground meat which cut down on preparation time. Leftover meats, thinly sliced, can be used. Add to the wok near the end of cooking time, just to warm through.

• Cut meat into thin, uniform slices or strips. Thinly slice vegetables on the diagonal to expose more surface for rapid heat penetration. This will cut down on cooking time and ensure even cooking. Group all the ingredients belonging to the same dish together.

• If marinating is required, marinate meat ahead and set aside - normally 15 to 30 minutes are adequate.

• House of Tsang offers several products great for marinades. Ginger Flavored Soy Sauce, Dark Soy Sauce, and Mandarin Marinade are pre-blended for easy marinating.

• Get the seasoning sauce or "gravy" ready by combining all ingredients in a bowl and set aside. (Stir again before adding to the wok as the cornstarch tends to settle.) If time is short, and you do not wish to hassle with all these ingredients, use one of the several House of Tsang stir fry sauces. They are ready for the discriminating cook to use right from the bottle, perfect every time.

• Have all the utensils - spatula, ladle, or wooden spoons, within easy reach.

Q. How do I plan a Chinese dinner party?

A. When planning a menu, look for a balance of flavors, textures, and colors for each dish. Observe the Yin and Yang philosophy. Contrast a spicy dish with a mild one; a crunchy-textured dish with a tender, succulent one; something light and fluffy

"Sharing a meal is the essence of a good friendship."

with something rich and hearty; and a sweet dish with one that's sour. Experiment with a variety of ingredients, sauces and condiments. Choose recipes to suit the season - light in summer, hearty in winter.

• Chinese food is designed for sharing, and the number of guests should determine the number of dishes to prepare. Usually one dish per one or two guests is sufficient, since everyone tries a small amount from each platter. Accompany any party menu with soup or some type of noodles and always a rice dish.

• Planning ahead lets you be a guest at your own party. Do all the pre-preparation like cutting and marinating the day before. Place each recipe's ingredients on separate trays, measured and set in order of use. It is a good idea to write a timetable coordinating each dish.

• To save time, plan a different cooking method for each dish. Have a slow-cooked dish in the oven, a steamed dish (which requires little attention), and a soup on the back burners. Rice can be prepared ahead in a saucepan or electric rice cooker, and a spicy noodle salad can be chilling in the refrigerator. Then at the last minute, you will have time to cook a couple of stir-fried dishes and still enjoy the meal with friends.

• Have a pot of green or oolong tea brewing for guests to enjoy after the meal. If you wish to serve wine, Johannisberg Riesling or dry Gewurztraminer compliment many Chinese dishes. Or, try the popular Shao Hsing rice wine, served warm like sake. Imported Chinese beer is also a good choice.

Q. How should I order in a restaurant?

A. Ordering a dinner in a Chinese restaurant is just as interesting and challenging as devising one at

Assortment of wine to be served warm (left to right): Shao Hsing wine, bottle of rice wine; sake; Mou Tai rice wine; green bamboo wine; rice wine; and Shao Hsing wine.

Assorted Chinese beer and wine.

Assorted teas (clockwise, from top): boxed Tuocha fermented tea; large disc of Po Nay fermented tea; Oolong tea; white chrysanthemum tea; jasmine tea; Chinese herb teas; and green tea with puffed rice.

"Kan pei means 'dry glass' in Chinese."

home. Once again, observe the Yin and Yang philosophy, which is basically "balance by contrast" - hot or cold, spicy or temperate, salty or bland.

• Choose one dish for each guest and ideally a dish from each food category - one from each of meat, fish, poultry, and vegetable, plus a soup.

• Try to have the dishes harmonize in color and to have a contrast of flavors - juicy steamed dumplings, spicy chicken with peanuts (Kung Pao), crunchy vegetables with slippery straw mushrooms, sweet & sour pork.

• Rice is always served or choose your favorite fried rice.

ORIENTAL BEVERAGES

Tea

Tea is the most common beverage in the Orient. It is served at all times and for almost every occasion.

Chinese prefer to serve fermented tea while Japanese usually favor unfermented tea. Both have elaborate tea ceremonies for weddings and other special celebrations. Here are the four major categories of tea:

• Green Tea: Unfermented tea such as Dragon Well has a natural bouquet and a pure and refreshing taste. It goes great with mild–flavored food.

• Semi-fermented Tea: Tea such as Oolong is a cross between green tea and fermented tea. It is popular in the United States as a daily tea.

• Fermented Tea: The most common ones are Lychee Red Tea and Iron Goddess of Mercy. Fermented tea produces a full body and a strong flavor. It is great served with heavy dishes and for sipping with dim sum.

• Scented Tea: Jasmine or Chrysanthemum Teas. A pleasant and fragrant aroma and after taste. A very light tea, especially good for beginning tea drinkers or as an after-dinner drink. A related category to scented tea is herbal tea, which is used for medicinal purposes. Many Oriental people drink it regularly to cleanse their systems.

People in the Orient prefer the pure taste of tea so milk or sweeteners are seldom used.

Wine and Beer

The Chinese word for wine is "chiew", and the Japanese is "sake". Most Oriental wines are fermented from grains of rice and barley and not from grapes. Their alcohol contents range from 40% to 65%. In the rest of the world, wines are fermented from grapes and have alcohol contents of 10% to 15%. Traditionally chiew and sake are served at room temperature or slightly warm.

Both China and Japan have been growing grapes and making Western-style wine for the last couple hundred years. And did you know that the famous Tsingtao beer was a German formulation started after the Boxer Rebellion? It ranks among the world's favorites.

Instant Impressions
Recipes for Less than 15 minutes

"I have no <u>time</u> to cook!" How often have you faced such a dilemma, not to mention such mundane choices as takeout from the local fast-food franchise or yet another frozen entree.

We've all experienced it. But now, there's a wonderful alternative. Let me show you the way to cook delightful, nutritional meals in about 15 minutes.

The Instant Impression recipes in this chapter are easy-to-prepare, delicious, and above all, quick. Many, such as mandarin chicken (page 50) or Laughing Clams (page 55) may be served as one-dish meals all by themselves. Others like Sanjook (page 66) or Gold Velvet (page 49) quickly become a meal when you add a salad or a steamed seasonal vegetable. Serve with a pot of tea or a glass of wine, and you're all set.

A hint for novice and experienced cooks alike: Don't forget to read through each recipe first and have all the ingredients on hand before you start cooking.

Garden Dynasty
(Fresh Vegetables with Spicy Dip)

Makes: 3/4 cup
Preparation time: 10 minutes

Cooking time: none

DIP

½   cup sour cream

¼   cup Classic Stir Fry Sauce *

2   teaspoons minced onion

2   teaspoons minced parsley

_____

About 1 pound (total weight) seasonal vegetables such as snow peas, broccoli and cauliflower flowerets, baby carrots, daikon and jicama strips, and cherry tomatoes

*   **House of Tsang Product**

1. Combine sour cream, stir fry sauce, onion, and parsley in a serving bowl and set aside.

2. Arrange vegetables in a basket or on a serving platter. Serve with dip.

Comments: Choose a variety of common and Oriental vegetables to make this a smashing party appetizer. Arrange the vegetables in a basket and alternate the colors and shapes. To add even more color, serve the dip in a "bowl" made from a cored red bell pepper or from a small head of purple cabbage that has been hollowed out. Serve at a buffet or garden party.

Singapore Sins
(Curry-flavored Deviled Eggs)

Makes: 8 appetizers
Preparation time: 10 minutes

Cooking time: none
Pictured on: Page 43

4   hard-cooked eggs

3   tablespoons mayonnaise

½   teaspoon Dijon-style mustard

1   teaspoon Singapore Curry Oil *

Cilantro (Chinese parsley), for garnish

*   **House of Tsang Product**

1. Peel eggs and slice in half lengthwise. Remove yolks, place in a bowl, and set egg white halves aside.

2. Mash yolks and add mayonnaise and mustard; stir until smooth and creamy. Blend in curry oil.

3. Mound filling into egg white halves with a table knife.

4. Garnish each with small cilantro leaves.

5. Transfer to serving platter. Chill until ready to serve.

Comments: These eggs are special enough to serve at a cocktail party. If you make the recipe in quantity, cook the eggs a day ahead and prepare the egg yolk filling. Refrigerate the filling and egg white halves separately, then assemble the eggs as needed. For a fancy presentation (see opposite page), use a pastry bag with a star tip to pipe in the filling. Sometimes I use small cooked shrimp or black sesame seeds as a garnish.

Black & White Pyramids
(Sesame-coated Cream Cheese Appetizers)

Makes: 12 servings
Preparation time: 10 minutes

Cooking time: 5 minutes
Pictured on: Page 43

1   package (8 oz.) cream
      cheese, chilled
3   tablespoons Korean
      Teriyaki Sauce *
⅓   cup white sesame seeds
⅓   cup black sesame seeds
1   thin-skinned (English)
      cucumber, cut into
      ⅛-inch thick slices

      Assorted crackers or
      thin slices of baguette

*   **House of Tsang Product**

1. Carefully, cut cream cheese in half crosswise; then cut each of those sections in half diagonally to form 4 triangles. Place them in a glass pie dish.

2. Pour teriyaki sauce over the cheese, turning the triangles to coat all sides. Let stand for about 5 minutes.

3. Meanwhile, in a wide frying pan, toast white sesame seeds over medium heat, shaking pan frequently, for 2 minutes or until seeds turn golden. Transfer to a sheet of waxed paper. Repeat procedure with black sesame seeds. (Because black sesame seeds don't change color, remove from heat when seeds smell toasty and aromatic.)

4. Lift cheese from marinade and gently roll 2 of the triangles in white sesame seeds, turning to coat all sides evenly. Repeat procedure with remaining cheese and black sesame seeds.

5. Place cheese triangles, pyramid-style, at one end of a serving platter or on a colorful lacquered tray. Arrange overlapping slices of cucumber around cheese. Tuck crackers or rounds of baguette near the cheese and provide a small knife for spreading. Serve at room temperature.

Comments: Delight unexpected guests with this tempting, easy-to-make appetizer. The combination of teriyaki-flavored cream cheese and sesame seeds is wonderful, and we think the presentation, especially when displayed on bright red lacquer, worthy of a most important occasion.

Fiery Roots of Spring

(Spicy Asparagus Appetizer)

Makes: 4 servings
Preparation time: 5 minutes

Cooking time: 4 minutes
Pictured on: Page 43

1 ½ pounds asparagus

SPICY SAUCE

2   tablespoons Spicy Brown
     Bean Sauce *

2   tablespoons cider
     vinegar

1 ½ tablespoons Wok Oil *

½   teaspoon minced fresh
     ginger

½   teaspoon sugar

*   **House of Tsang Product**

1. Snap off and discard tough ends of asparagus.

2. Blanch asparagus in boiling water for 4 minutes or until crisp-tender; refresh under cold water to retain the color and stop the cooking. Drain and set aside.

3. Combine brown bean sauce, vinegar, wok oil, ginger, and sugar; pour into a small serving bowl.

4. Place asparagus on a serving platter or 4 small individual plates. Offer sauce alongside platter for dipping or spoon sauce over individual servings. Serve at room temperature as an appetizer or first course.

Comments: Tender, young spears of asparagus go perfectly with our Spicy Brown Bean Sauce. Here's an easy way to remove tough white asparagus ends. Hold the root end in one hand and grab the middle of the asparagus with the other hand. Bend the stalk and with one quick motion, the tough part breaks off.

A trio of tempting appetizers include (clockwise): Singapore Sins (curry-flavored deviled eggs with cilantro), Black & White Pyramids (cream cheese triangles coated with toasted black and white sesame seeds), and Fiery Roots of Spring (blanched whole asparagus with a spicy sauce for dipping).

Emerald Bonsai
(Broccoli with Oyster Sauce)

Makes: 2 servings
Preparation time: 5 minutes

Cooking time: 4 minutes

2	teaspoons Wok Oil *
½	onion, thinly sliced
4	cups broccoli flowerets
¼	cup chicken broth
2	tablespoons oyster sauce
½	teaspoon Hot Chili Sesame Oil *

1. Place a wok or large skillet over high heat until hot. Add wok oil, swirling to coat sides of pan.
2. Add onion; stir-fry for 30 seconds.
3. Add broccoli; stir-fry for 30 seconds. Add chicken broth; cover and cook for 2½ minutes or until broccoli is crisp-tender.
4. Add oyster sauce and chili sesame oil; toss and cook until evenly coated and heated through.

* **House of Tsang Product**

Comments: Serve this wonderful vegetable side dish with grilled fish such as our Bronze Swimmer (page 58) or with any chicken dish. Hot Chili Sesame Oil gives this simple dish a unique, zesty touch.

Seasonal Harvest
(Stir-fried Seasonal Vegetables)

Makes: 2 servings
Preparation time: 8 minutes

Cooking time: 4 minutes

2   teaspoons Wok Oil *

¼   pound snow peas, ends
     and strings removed

1   cup sliced mushrooms

1   red bell pepper, seeded
     and cut into julienne
     strips

1   can (8 oz.) sliced
     bamboo shoots, drained

¼   cup chicken broth

1   teaspoon Hot Chili
     Sesame Oil *

*   **House of Tsang Product**

1. Place a wok or large skillet over high heat until hot. Add wok oil, swirling to coat sides of pan.

2. Add snow peas; stir-fry for 30 seconds. Stir in mushrooms, bell pepper, bamboo shoots, and chicken broth; cook for 3 minutes or until vegetables are crisp-tender.

3. Stir in chili sesame oil. Serve immediately.

Comments: Use this recipe when you want an easy vegetable dish to accompany grilled chicken or fish. If you use another vegetable in place of one listed above (such as substituting zucchini for snow peas), just remember to cut the vegetable into pieces of the same size and shape so they will cook evenly.

Marinated boneless chicken, slices of carrot and onion, tender baby corn and fancy-cut snow peas create a striking contrast in this quick to prepare stir-fry dish called Szechuan Fowl Play.

Szechuan Fowl Play

(Spicy Chicken & Vegetables)

Makes: 2 servings
Preparation time: 8 minutes

Cooking time: 5 minutes
Pictured on: Page 46

¾ pound boneless chicken breasts

1 tablespoon Mandarin Marinade *

2 tablespoons Wok Oil *

½ onion, thinly sliced

1 carrot, cut diagonally into thin slices

2 tablespoons chicken broth

6 ears canned baby corn

2 ounces snow peas, ends and strings removed

2 tablespoons Szechuan Spicy Stir Fry Sauce *

* **House of Tsang Product**

1. Remove skin from chicken and cut meat into thin slices. Place in a bowl with marinade and set aside.

2. Place a wok or large skillet over high heat until hot. Add 1½ tablespoons of the wok oil, swirling to coat sides of pan.

3. Add chicken; stir-fry for 2 minutes or until chicken turns opaque. Remove chicken from wok and set aside.

4. Add remaining ½ tablespoon wok oil. When oil is hot, add onion, carrot, and chicken broth. Cover and cook for 1 minute or until vegetables are crisp-tender.

5. Return chicken to wok. Stir in corn, snow peas, and stir fry sauce. Cook for 1 minute or until heated through.

Comments: This colorful, spicy dish is perfect for everyday meals - winter or summer.

Rice In A Rush

(Classic Chinese Fried Rice)

Makes: 2 to 3 servings
Preparation time: 6 minutes

Cooking time: 4 minutes

2   tablespoons Wok Oil *
½   cup diced cooked ham
1   cup frozen peas and diced carrots, thawed
2   green onions (including tops), thinly sliced
4   cups cooked long-grain rice
¼   cup Classic Stir Fry Sauce *
2   tablespoons chicken broth
1   cup shredded iceberg lettuce

*   **House of Tsang Product**

1. Place a wok or large skillet over high heat until hot. Add wok oil, swirling to coat sides of pan.

2. Add ham, peas and carrots, and green onions; stir-fry for 1 minute.

3. Stir in rice, breaking up clumps with a spoon. Add stir fry sauce and chicken broth. Cook and toss for 2 minutes or until rice is heated through.

4. Stir in lettuce; cook for 30 seconds.

Comments: When served with a salad, this ham and vegetable fried rice dish makes a quick, tasty meal. Don't throw out your leftover rice. Rice In A Rush is actually easier to prepare with day-old rice because the grains separate more easily when stir-fried.

Gold Velvet
(Creamy Corn & Crab Soup)

Makes: 4 servings
Preparation time: 5 minutes

Cooking time: 4 minutes

¼   cup sliced water chestnuts

2   cups chicken broth

1   can (8¾ oz.) cream-style corn

⅓   cup frozen peas, thawed

¼   pound crab meat, flaked

1   teaspoon Hot Chili Sesame Oil *

*   **House of Tsang Product**

1. Coarsely chop water chestnuts; set aside.

2. Bring chicken broth to a boil in a 2-quart saucepan. Stir in corn, peas, and water chestnuts; cook for 2 minutes. Add crab and heat through.

3. Stir in chili sesame oil.

Comments: Full-flavored and satisfying, this delicious soup has the consistency of New England clam chowder. If fresh crab is not available, you can use surimi (imitation) crab meat. It tastes remarkably close to the real thing.

Mandarin Treasure

(Sweet & Sour Chicken with Oranges)

Makes: 2 servings
Preparation time: 8 minutes

Cooking time: 3 minutes
Pictured on: Page 51

⅔   pound boneless chicken breasts

1½   tablespoons Mandarin Marinade *

2   tablespoons Wok Oil *

½   cup sliced water chestnuts

⅓   cup Sweet & Sour Stir Fry Sauce *

¼   teaspoon crushed red pepper

1   can (11 oz.) mandarin oranges, drained

3   green onions (including tops), cut into 2-inch slivers

*   **House of Tsang Product**

1. Remove skin from chicken and cut meat into bite-size pieces. Place in a bowl with marinade and set aside.

2. Place a wok or large skillet over high heat until hot. Add wok oil, swirling to coat sides of pan.

3. Add chicken; stir-fry for 2 minutes or until chicken turns opaque.

4. Add water chestnuts, stir fry sauce, and crushed red pepper; cook for 1 minute. Gently stir in half of the mandarin oranges and half of the green onions.

5. Transfer to a serving platter. Garnish with remaining mandarin oranges and green onions.

Comments: One of my all-time favorites!

Pieces of chicken, sliced water chestnuts, and mandarin orange segments highlight this spicy sweet and sour dish garnished with slivered green onion and bits of crushed red pepper. Serve Mandarin Treasure with hot, steamed rice.

Turkey Bundles

(Lettuce-wrapped Turkey & Vegetables)

Makes: 2 servings
Preparation time: 10 minutes

Cooking time: 4 minutes

¼   cup sliced water chestnuts

1 ½ tablespoons Wok Oil *

½   pound ground turkey

½   red bell pepper, seeded
and diced

1   zucchini, diced

1   green onion (including
top), finely chopped

3   tablespoons Korean
Teriyaki Sauce *

8   butter lettuce leaves

1. Coarsely chop water chestnuts; set aside.

2. Place a wok or large skillet over high heat until hot. Add wok oil, swirling to coat sides of pan.

3. Add turkey; stir-fry for 2 minutes or until lightly browned.

4. Add water chestnuts, bell pepper, zucchini, green onion, and teriyaki sauce; stir-fry for 2 minutes.

5. To serve, place 1 heaping tablespoon of turkey mixture in the center of a lettuce leaf, wrap like a burrito, and eat out of hand.

*   **House of Tsang Product**

Comments: When you want something that's simple to make and fun to serve, offer your guests or family teriyaki-flavored turkey. Here, we've combined ground turkey, water chestnuts, on-ions, and other vegetables to create our own Oriental version of a burrito.

Chicken Power

(Curried Chicken & Tofu)

Makes: 2 servings
Preparation time: 8 minutes

Cooking time: 5 minutes

⅔ pound boneless chicken
    breasts

1½ tablespoons Wok Oil *

2   cups sliced mushrooms

½   cup frozen peas, thawed

3   green onions (including
    tops), cut diagonally
    into 1½-inch pieces

8   ounces firm tofu,
    drained and cut into
    1½-inch cubes

3   tablespoons Classic Stir
    Fry Sauce *

1   tablespoon Singapore
    Curry Oil *

* **House of Tsang Product**

1. Remove skin from chicken and cut meat into bite-size pieces.

2. Place a wok or large skillet over high heat until hot. Add wok oil, swirling to coat sides of pan.

3. Add chicken; stir-fry for 2 minutes or until chicken turns opaque.

4. Add mushrooms and peas; cook for 30 seconds. Add green onions, tofu, stir fry sauce, and curry oil. Cook for 1 minute or until heated through.

Comments: High in protein, yet low in calories and cholesterol, tofu is the fitness food for the 80's. Serve Chicken Power with steamed rice and sliced cucumbers marinated in seasoned rice vinegar.

For a delicious variation, substitute the House of Tsang Mongolian Fire Oil or Hot Chili Sesame Oil for curry oil.

Fresh succulent clams, flavored with spicy brown bean sauce and white wine, nestle in a hearty broth brimming with Chinese noodles. Ladle Laughing Clams into earthenware bowls and garnish with additional minced parsley to serve.

Laughing Clams
(Clams with Spicy Brown Bean Sauce)

Makes: 4 servings
Preparation time: 6 minutes

Cooking time: 5 to 7 minutes
Pictured on: Page 54

1   tablespoon Wok Oil *

1   onion, chopped

1   cup dry white wine

1   cup chicken broth

2   tablespoons Spicy Brown
    Bean Sauce *

3   tablespoons chopped
    parsley

2   pounds hard-shell clams
    or mussels, scrubbed

1   teaspoon Hot Chili
    Sesame Oil *

2   cups cooked rice or
    noodles

    Additional chopped
    parsley, for garnish

*   **House of Tsang Product**

1. Place a 5-quart pan over medium heat until hot.
    Add wok oil, swirling to coat bottom of pan.

2. Add onion; cook for 3 minutes or until translu-
    cent. Stir in wine, chicken broth, brown bean
    sauce, and parsley.

3. Add clams and bring to a boil, then reduce heat.
    Cover and simmer for 5 minutes or until shells
    open. (Discard any clams that don't open.) Stir
    in chili sesame oil.

4. To serve, divide rice or noodles evenly among 4
    large bowls. Arrange clams on top. Ladle broth
    evenly over clams. Top each with a sprinkling of
    extra parsley.

Comments: Enjoy this hearty, one-dish meal
anytime. When purchasing clams or mussels,
make sure they are tightly closed. This indicates
they are alive. After cooking, the shells will open.
Discard any that remain tightly closed.

South China Sea Catch

(Fish Fillet with Spicy Brown Bean Sauce)

Makes: 4 servings
Preparation time: 5 minutes

Cooking time: 6 to 8 minutes

2   tablespoon Mandarin Marinade *

2   tablespoons Spicy Brown Bean Sauce *

1   pound firm white fish fillets (such as snapper or rock cod), each about ¾-inch thick

2   green onions (including tops), cut into 2-inch slivers

1   tablespoon slivered fresh ginger

*   **House of Tsang Product**

1. Combine marinade and brown bean sauce in a small bowl. Brush mixture evenly over fish fillets.

2. Place fillets in a single layer in a heatproof dish. Sprinkle evenly with green onions and ginger slivers. Cover dish tightly with foil.

3. Bake in a 450°F oven for 6 to 8 minutes or until fish turns opaque and just begins to flake.

Comments: Kick back and relax because this wonderful recipe takes care of itself. Baking will vary according to the thickness of fish. A rule of thumb: Allow 10 minutes for every inch thickness of fish. Serve with your favorite rice and steamed seasonal vegetables.

Fish Fillet Olé
(Salsa-topped Fish Fillets)

Makes: 4 servings
Preparation time: 6 minutes

Cooking time: 6 to 7 minutes

SALSA

1   tomato, chopped

3   green onions (including tops), thinly sliced

2   tablespoons red wine vinegar

1   tablespoon Ginger Flavored Soy Sauce *

1   teaspoon Hot Chili Sesame Oil *

———

1½ pounds firm white fish fillets (such as snapper or swordfish), each about ¾-inch thick

2   teaspoons Wok Oil *

2   tablespoons Szechuan Spicy Stir Fry Sauce *

* **House of Tsang Product**

1. Combine tomato, green onions, vinegar, soy sauce, and chili sesame oil in a bowl; mix well. Let stand while you cook the fish.

2. Preheat broiler and adjust rack so fish will be 3 to 4 inches from heat.

3. Combine wok oil and stir fry sauce; brush on both sides of fillets. Place fish on a rack in a foil-lined broiling pan.

4. Place under heat and broil for 3 minutes. Turn fish over and broil for 3 to 4 more minutes or until fish turns opaque and just begins to flake.

5. To serve, arrange fish on a serving platter and top each fillet with a generous serving of salsa.

Comments: Fresh chilies (the hotter the better) are a typical ingredient in salsa. But this recipe incorporates hot chili sesame oil for punch instead. Our salsa is excellent on grilled hamburgers or broiled chicken, too. Serve with a glass of cold beer.

Bronze Swimmer

(Teriyaki Salmon Steaks)

Makes: 4 servings
Preparation time: 5 minutes

Cooking time: 6 to 8 minutes
Pictured on: Page 59

1 teaspoon Hot Chili Sesame Oil *

¼ cup Korean Teriyaki Sauce *

1½ pounds salmon steaks, each about ¾-inch thick

1 green onion (including top), cut into 2-inch slivers

* **House of Tsang Product**

1. Preheat broiler and adjust rack so fish will be 3 to 4 inches from heat.

2. Combine chili sesame oil and teriyaki sauce in a small bowl. Brush sauce evenly over both sides of salmon. Place fish on a rack in a foil-lined broiling pan.

3. Place under heat and broil for 3 minutes. Turn fish over and broil for 3 to 4 more minutes or until salmon turns opaque and just begins to flake.

4. Garnish with green onion slivers.

Comments: If you love salmon, this fabulous and simple dish is for you! Teriyaki is a trademark dish in Japan and literally means "glaze broiled". Other Asian countries adopted the usage, adding spices indigenous to their region. Our teriyaki features spices traditionally used in Korean cooking.

Garnished with slivers of green onion, thin slices of cucumber and a festive onion brush, grilled teriyaki-flavored salmon steak makes a spectacular presentation. Serve additional sauce, seasoned with Hot Chili Sesame Oil, alongside our Bronze Swimmer.

Fowl For All Seasons
(Turkey Teriyaki Stir-fry)

Makes: 2 servings
Preparation time: 6 minutes

Cooking time: 5 minutes

¾ pound boneless turkey breast

1½ tablespoons Wok Oil *

1 zucchini, thinly sliced

½ onion, thinly sliced

3 tablespoons Korean Teriyaki Sauce *

* **House of Tsang Product**

1. Remove skin from turkey and cut meat into thin strips approximately ½-inch wide and 2-inches long. Set aside.

2. Place a wok or large skillet over high heat until hot. Add wok oil, swirling to coat sides of pan.

3. Add turkey; stir-fry for 2 minutes or until turkey is lightly browned.

4. Add zucchini, onion, and teriyaki sauce; cover and cook for 3 minutes or until vegetables are crisp-tender.

Comments: Looking for an unusual way to serve turkey? Here's a quick and foolproof dish guaranteed to please the entire family. You'll find boneless turkey breasts in most supermarkets or, if you wish, purchase a turkey breast half and bone it yourself.

Emperor's Good Fortune
(Turkey Rice Salad)

Makes: 4 servings
Preparation time: 10 minutes

Cooking time: 5 minutes

¼   cup slivered almonds

DRESSING

¼   cup mayonnaise
3   tablespoons Classic Stir
Fry Sauce *

SALAD

2   cups cooked long-grain
rice
1½ cups diced cooked
turkey
1   carrot, shredded
½   red bell pepper, seeded
and diced
2   green onions (including
tops), thinly sliced

Butter lettuce leaves

*   **House of Tsang Product**

1. Preheat oven to 350°F. Spread almonds in a shallow baking pan and bake in preheated oven for 5 minutes or until golden brown. Set aside.

2. Combine mayonnaise and stir fry sauce in a small bowl and set aside.

3. Combine rice, turkey, carrot, bell pepper, and green onions in a large bowl. Add dressing and toss well.

4. To serve, arrange lettuce leaves on 4 individual salad plates. Divide the salad among the plates and sprinkle each with 1 tablespoon toasted almonds.

Comments: This turkey rice salad is very non-Chinese, but it is one of my favorites. I can serve it any time.

Colorful strips of three kinds of pepper are stir-fried with thin slices of spicy beef and onion in just minutes. Offer Belles & Beef with bowls of steamed rice.

Belles & Beef

(Three Pepper Flank Steak)

Makes: 2 servings
Preparation time: 6 minutes

Cooking time: 9 minutes
Pictured on: Page 62

½ pound beef sirloin or flank steak

3 tablespoons Szechuan Spicy Stir Fry Sauce *

1 ½ tablespoons Wok Oil *

1 green bell pepper, seeded and cut into julienne strips

1 red bell pepper, seeded and cut into julienne strips

1 yellow bell pepper, seeded and cut into julienne strips

1 onion, thinly sliced

* **House of Tsang Product**

1. Slice beef across the grain into thin, slanting slices. Combine beef and 1 tablespoon of the stir fry sauce in a bowl; stir to coat. Set aside.

2. Place a wok or large skillet over high heat until hot. Add wok oil, swirling to coat sides of pan.

3. Add beef; stir-fry for 2 minutes or until barely pink. Remove beef from wok and set aside.

4. Add bell peppers and onion. Toss and cook for 5 minutes or until vegetables are crisp-tender.

5. Return beef to wok. Stir in remaining 2 tablespoons stir fry sauce and cook for 30 seconds or until heated through.

Comments: Guests love the colorful presentation of our stir-fried beef with three peppers. Or, for hot-sandwich fans, try serving it in soft French rolls or even rolled up in a warm flour tortilla — fajita-style.

Blue Plate Special
(Tomato Beef)

Makes: 2 servings
Preparation time: 8 minutes

Cooking time: 4 minutes

½ pound beef sirloin or flank steak

1 tablespoon Mandarin Marinade *

1½ tablespoons Wok Oil *

1 green bell pepper, seeded and cut into ¾-inch squares

½ onion, cut into wedges

2 firm tomatoes, each cut into 8 wedges

½ cup pineapple chunks

3 tablespoons Sweet & Sour Stir Fry Sauce *

* **House of Tsang Product**

1. Slice beef across the grain into thin slanting slices. Place in a bowl with marinade and set aside.

2. Place a wok or large skillet over high heat until hot. Add 1 tablespoon of the wok oil, swirling to coat sides of pan.

3. Add beef; stir-fry for 2 minutes or until barely pink. Remove beef from wok and set aside.

4. Add remaining ½ tablespoon wok oil. When oil is hot, add bell pepper and onion; cook for 1 minute or until vegetables are crisp-tender.

5. Return beef to wok. Stir in tomatoes, pineapple chunks, and stir fry sauce. Cook for 1 minute or until heated through.

Comments: Hearty, satisfying, and easy to prepare, Tomato Beef may become a family favorite.

Steak Oriental
(Steak with Classic Stir Fry Sauce)

Makes: 4 servings
Preparation time: 5 minutes

Cooking time: 8 to 10 minutes

2   tablespoons Classic Stir
    Fry Sauce *

1   teaspoon Hot Chili
    Sesame Oil *

2   pounds beef loin,
    T-bone, or New York
    steaks, about ¾-inch
    thick

*   **House of Tsang Product**

1. Combine stir fry sauce and chili sesame oil in a small bowl.

2. Brush steaks with 1 tablespoon sauce mixture; marinate for 5 minutes.

3. Preheat broiler and adjust rack so beef will be 3 to 4 inches from heat.

4. Place meat on a rack in a foil-lined broiling pan. Place under heat and broil, brushing occasionally with the remaining sauce mixture, for 4 to 5 minutes on each side for medium-rare.

Comments: When you crave the flavor of barbecued meat, try grilling this on a small hibachi or on a gas or electric barbecue. Grilled sliced eggplant and shoestring potatoes are great side dishes.

Sanjook

(Skewered Beef & Green Onions)

Makes: 4 servings
Preparation time: 9 minutes

Cooking time: 4 minutes
Pictured on: Page 67

1   pound boneless top
     sirloin or New York
     steak, about 1½ inches
     thick

¼   cup Korean Teriyaki
     Sauce *

1   teaspoon Mongolian
     Fire Oil *

8   green onions (including
     tops), cut into 1½-inch
     pieces

* **House of Tsang Product**

1. Preheat broiler and adjust rack so beef will be
    3 to 4 inches from heat.

2. Slice beef across the grain into slices about
    ¼-inch thick. Each slice should measure ap-
    proximately ¼ x 1½ x 2 inches.

3. Combine teriyaki sauce and fire oil in a small
    bowl and set aside.

4. Alternately thread beef and green onions on 8-
    inch metal or presoaked bamboo skewers,
    keeping meat slightly flat. Brush both sides
    with 3 tablespoons of the sauce mixture.

5. Place skewers on a rack in a foil-lined broiling
    pan. Place under heat and broil for 2 minutes.
    Turn meat over and brush with the remaining
    1 tablespoon sauce mixture. Continue to broil
    for 2 more minutes (for medium-rare) or until
    meat is done to your liking. You may also cook
    Sanjook on a barbecue grill about 4 inches
    above a solid bed of low glowing coals.

Comments: Here's a tip to prevent the ends of
bamboo skewers from burning. Soak them in
water for 15 minutes before threading with
meat and onions. Koreans usually serve Sanjook with rice and kim chee, a hot garlicky
relish available in Oriental markets. For picnic
fare, slide the grilled meat and onions off the
skewer and serve in pocket bread.

Skewers of teriyaki-flavored beef and green onion grill on a tabletop hibachi or outdoor barbecue in just minutes. Treat guests to an Oriental version of the Mexican specialty by serving Sanjook wrapped in hot, flour tortillas, "fajita-style."

Family Fare

(Pork & Summer Vegetables)

Makes: 2 servings
Preparation time: 8 minutes

Cooking time: 5 minutes

¾   pound lean boneless pork

2   tablespoons Mandarin Marinade *

2   tablespoons Wok Oil *

1   carrot, thinly sliced

2   zucchini, roll-cut about ½-inch thick

½   onion, cut into 1-inch squares

¼   cup Classic Stir Fry Sauce *

2   tablespoons water

*   **House of Tsang Product**

1. Slice pork into thin slices approximately ½-inch wide and 2-inches long. Place in a bowl with marinade and set aside.

2. Place a wok or large skillet over high heat until hot. Add wok oil, swirling to coat sides of pan.

3. Add pork; stir-fry for 2 minutes or until lightly browned.

4. Add carrot, zucchini, onion, stir fry sauce, and water; cover and cook for 2 minutes or until carrot is crisp-tender.

Comments: Simple, fresh ingredients highlight this classic stir-fry favorite. Serve it over fresh pasta or Chinese egg noodles.

Mixed Media
(Fruit Salad With Sweet & Sour Dressing)

Makes: 4 servings
Preparation time: 8 minutes

Cooking time: none

½   cup plain yogurt

3   tablespoons Sweet & Sour Stir Fry Sauce *

2   teaspoons brown sugar

⅛   teaspoon ground cinnamon

4   cups sliced fresh fruit and berries, such as honeydew melon, apples, kiwi, pineapple, and strawberries or canned Oriental fruit, such as lychees and mandarin oranges

Sprigs of mint or small fresh edible flowers, for garnish

1. Combine yogurt, stir fry sauce, brown sugar, and cinnamon in a small bowl; set aside.

2. On a large glass plate, arrange slices of melon, apples, kiwi, pineapple, and whole berries.

3. Spoon some of the dressing over the fruit.

4. Garnish plate with sprigs of mint (or flowers) and pass remaining dressing at the table.

Comments: By combining the tangy taste of yogurt with our own sweet and sour sauce, we've created one of the simplest recipes to prepare when you want an unusual, easy-to-make dressing for fresh fruit salad.

*   **House of Tsang Product**

Timely Temptations
Recipes for Less than 30 minutes

Today you have a little more time to think about dinner, perhaps up to a half an hour to spare. But what can cook in half an hour?

I say "plenty." Thirty minutes is enough time to marinate meat, soak exotic mushrooms, and even deep-fry Tempura (page 87).

Many recipes in this chapter, such as Sweet & Sour Pork (page 98) and Tangy Bird (page 82) benefit by the addition of freshly cooked noodles or steamed rice. So the first thing to do when you walk into the kitchen is start boiling a pot of water, if you want noodles, or set a pot of rice to cook on the stove before doing anything else.

Our Timely Temptations will tempt you even if you have more than half an hour to cook. For a sumptuous meal, enjoy them anytime.

Golden Triangles
(Shrimp Toast)

Makes: 16 appetizers
Preparation time: 15 minutes

Cooking time: 10 minutes

MARINADE

1 egg white

2 teaspoons dry sherry

1 teaspoon Pure Sesame Seed Oil *

2 teaspoons cornstarch

¼ teaspoon salt

⅛ teaspoon white pepper

¼ pound crab meat, flaked

¼ pound medium-size raw shrimp, shelled, de-veined, and coarsely chopped

¼ cup sliced water chest-nuts, coarsely chopped

1 thin slice ham, coarsely chopped

1 green onion (including top), thinly sliced

8 slices day-old firm white bread

Vegetable oil for deep-frying

* **House of Tsang Product**

1. Combine marinade ingredients in a medium bowl. Add crab meat and shrimp; stir to coat. Set aside for 10 minutes.

2. Place crab-shrimp mixture, water chestnuts, ham, and green onion in a food processor. Process for 15 seconds or until mixture is well blended but still slightly lumpy. To make without a processor, chop ingredients with a heavy knife until blended.

3. Trim crusts from bread. Cut each slice diagonally to make 2 triangles. Spread about 1 tablespoon mixture over each bread triangle.

4. Set wok in a ring stand and add vegetable oil to a depth of about 2 inches. Place over high heat until oil reaches 350°F. on a deep-frying ther-mometer. Add triangles, shrimp side down, a few at a time. Deep-fry for 1 minute; turn, and cook for 30 seconds or until filling is cooked through. Lift out triangles with a slotted spoon and drain on paper towels.

5. Transfer to a serving platter.

Comments: Since you will be cooking the shrimp triangles in batches, have a 200°F. oven hot to keep the first triangles warm while cooking the remaining ones.

Ming Coins
(Veal-filled Mushroom Caps)

Makes: 16 appetizers
Preparation time: 15 minutes

Cooking time: 15 minutes

FILLING

½   pound ground veal

1   egg, lightly beaten

2   green onions (including tops), minced

2   tablespoons Ginger Flavored Soy Sauce *

1   teaspoon chopped cilantro (Chinese parsley)

1 ½   teaspoons cornstarch

---

16   large mushrooms, stems removed

1   tablespoon Hot Chili Sesame Oil *

Additional cilantro sprigs (Chinese parsley), for garnish

*   **House of Tsang Product**

1. Combine filling ingredients in a bowl and mix well.

2. Lightly brush mushroom caps with chili sesame oil.

3. Stuff each mushroom cap with filling mixture, forming a smooth mound.

4. Place stuffed mushrooms, filling side up, in a large baking pan. Bake in a 400°F. oven for 15 minutes or until cooked through. Serve hot. Garnish plate with cilantro sprigs.

Comments: A spoonful of ginger-flavored veal and onion mixture nestles inside each large mushroom cap. They are perfect appetizers that can be made several hours ahead of time for your next get-together.

Spicy Spuds

(Chili-flavored Potato Salad)

Makes: 4 servings
Preparation time: 20 minutes

Cooking time: 5 minutes

DRESSING

½	cup mayonnaise
¼	cup rice vinegar
2	tablespoons Mongolian Fire Oil *
1	tablespoon Hot Chili Sesame Oil *
1	teaspoon sugar
½	teaspoon salt

1½	pounds russet potatoes, peeled and cut into ¾-inch cubes
3	strips bacon, cooked and crumbled
1	can (2¼ oz.) sliced ripe olives, drained
2	tablespoons chopped parsley
2	tablespoons finely chopped onion

* **House of Tsang Product**

1. Combine dressing ingredients in a small bowl and set aside.

2. In a medium saucepan, boil potatoes in enough water to cover for 5 minutes or until tender when pierced with a fork. Drain and place potatoes in a large salad bowl; let cool until lukewarm.

3. Add dressing ingredients, bacon, olives, parsley, and onion. Gently toss to coat potatoes evenly. Serve at room temperature or chill before serving.

Comments: Here's a perfect marriage of Eastern flavors and Western ingredients. This Oriental-style potato salad makes a delicious accompaniment to Beijing Burgers (page 92).

Rice To The Occasion

(Deluxe Fried Rice)

Makes: 4 servings
Preparation time: 20 minutes

Cooking time: 8 minutes
Pictured on: Page 75

1   egg, lightly beaten

SEASONING MIXTURE

¼   cup chicken broth

2   tablespoons Dark Soy Sauce *

1   tablespoon Pure Sesame Seed Oil *

½   teaspoon sugar

⅛   teaspoon white pepper

---

2   tablespoons Wok Oil *

¼   cup chopped onion

2   ounces snow peas, ends and strings removed, cut in half crosswise

2   ounces small cooked shrimp

¼   pound barbecued pork or cooked chicken, cut into ½-inch cubes

4   cups cooked long-grain rice

*   **House of Tsang Product**

1. Place a 6-inch frying pan with a nonstick finish over medium-high heat until hot. Pour in egg, tilting pan to coat bottom evenly. Cook just until egg is set and feels dry on top. Remove omelet from pan and let cool slightly. Roll up omelet like a jelly roll. Slice crosswise into ½-inch thick strips, then cut strips into ½-inch squares.

2. Combine seasoning mixture in a small bowl and set aside.

3. Place a wok or large skillet over high heat until hot. Add wok oil, swirling to coat sides of pan.

4. Add onion; cook for 10 seconds. Add snow peas; stir-fry for 30 seconds.

5. Add seasoning mixture, shrimp, and pork; cook for 1 minute.

6. Stir in rice, breaking up clumps with a spoon. Cook and toss for 3 minutes or until rice is heated through.

7. Remove from heat. Add egg squares and toss to mix.

Comments: For an attractive molded presentation, spray a 6-cup mold with a nonstick cooking spray. Line the bottom with the shrimp and arrange pork, egg squares, and snow peas along the sides. Fill with the cooked rice mixture, patting firmly into the mold. Unmold onto a serving platter. Garnish the top with a few small cooked shrimp.

Ordinary fried rice it's not! Cooked rice, seasoned with sesame oil and soy, is molded in a bowl already decorated with tiny shrimp, bits of egg and barbecued pork, snow peas and chopped onion. We call it Rice To The Occasion.

East-West Omelet

(Vegetable Omelet)

Makes: 4 servings
Preparation time: 15 minutes

Cooking time: 10 minutes

2 tablespoons Wok Oil *

2 carrots, cut into match-stick pieces

2 ounces snow peas, ends and strings removed, cut into matchstick pieces

8 mushrooms, thinly sliced

1 red or yellow bell pepper, seeded and cut into matchstick pieces

2 green onions (including tops), cut into 2-inch slivers

2 tablespoons water

3 tablespoons Korean Teriyaki Sauce *

1 tablespoon Ginger Flavored Soy Sauce *

1 teaspoon Hot Chili Sesame Oil *

2 teaspoons cornstarch mixed with 4 teaspoons water

8 eggs, beaten

1. Place a wok or large skillet over high heat until hot. Add 1 tablespoon of the wok oil, swirling to coat sides of pan. Add carrots; cook for 1 minute or until crisp-tender. Add snow peas, mushrooms, bell pepper, green onions, and water; cook for 1 minute or until snow peas are crisp-tender.

2. Add teriyaki sauce, soy sauce, and chili sesame oil; cook for 1 minute. Add cornstarch solution and cook, stirring, until sauce boils and thickens slightly. Keep warm.

3. Place a 7 to 8-inch omelet pan with a nonstick finish over medium-high heat until hot. Add ¾ teaspoon of the wok oil, swirling to coat bottom of pan. Pour in ¼ of the eggs all at once. As edges begin to set, lift with a spatula and tilt pan to let uncooked egg flow underneath. When egg no longer flows freely, place one-fourth of the vegetable filling on one side of the omelet and fold in half. Keep warm in a 200°F. oven. Repeat with remaining eggs and filling to make 3 more omelets.

* **House of Tsang Product**

Naked Noodles
(Sesame Noodles)

Makes: 4 servings
Preparation time: 15 minutes

Cooking time: 5 minutes

2   tablespoons sesame seeds
1   pound fresh Chinese noodles
1   tablespoon Hot Chili Sesame Oil *

DRESSING

¼   cup peanut butter
¼   cup rice vinegar
3   tablespoons Ginger Flavored Soy Sauce *
1   tablespoon Mongolian Fire Oil *
2   teaspoons sugar

————————

3   green onions (including tops), cut into 2-inch slivers
2   tablespoons chopped, roasted peanuts

1. In a wide frying pan, toast sesame seeds over medium heat, shaking pan frequently, for 2 minutes or until seeds turn golden. Remove and set aside.

2. Cook noodles according to package directions until tender but firm to the bite. Drain well and toss with chili sesame oil. Transfer noodles to a serving bowl.

3. Combine dressing ingredients in a small saucepan. Cook, stirring constantly, over medium-high heat for 1½ minutes; pour over noodles. Add sesame seeds, green onions, and chopped peanuts; toss well.

4. Serve warm or at room temperature.

Comments: For a meal that's easy on the cook, serve sesame noodles with Flower Drums (page 84) and shredded Chinese (napa) cabbage dressed with seasoned rice vinegar.

*   **House of Tsang Product**

Szechuan Noodle Toss is a visual display of freshly-cooked egg noodles, spicy lean ground pork, and matchstick pieces of green onion and carrot. Bring to the table in a beautiful bowl (as pictured), then toss thoroughly just before serving.

Szechuan Noodle Toss

(Spicy Noodles with Minced Pork)

Makes: 4 servings
Preparation time: 20 minutes

Cooking time: 4 minutes
Pictured on: Page 78

½ pound lean ground pork

1 tablespoon Mandarin Marinade *

12 ounces fresh Chinese noodles

2 teaspoons Pure Sesame Seed Oil *

1½ tablespoons Wok Oil *

¼ cup Szechuan Spicy Stir Fry Sauce *

2 green onions (including tops), cut into 2-inch slivers

1 carrot, cut into matchstick pieces

* **House of Tsang Product**

1. Combine pork and marinade in a small bowl. Set aside for 15 minutes.

2. Cook noodles according to package directions until tender but firm to the bite. Drain well and toss with sesame oil. Transfer noodles to a serving bowl.

3. Place a wok or large skillet over high heat until hot. Add wok oil, swirling to coat sides of pan. Add pork; stir-fry for 3 minutes or until browned. Add stir fry sauce and cook for 1 minute or until heated through.

4. Pour meat mixture over noodles. Arrange green onions and carrot over noodles. At the table, toss lightly so all noodles are coated with sauce.

Comments: You may substitute 8 ounces dried egg noodles or spaghetti for the fresh Chinese ones. Chinese egg noodles come in a variety of widths, just like Italian pasta, so choose your favorite size.

East-West Salad

(Fresh Seafood & Melon Salad)

Makes: 6 servings
Preparation time: 25 minutes

Cooking time: 2 minutes

DRESSING

¼	cup rice vinegar
2	tablespoons Ginger Flavored Soy Sauce *
2	tablespoons sugar
2	tablespoons Pure Sesame Seed Oil*
2	teaspoons Dijon-style mustard
1	teaspoon Mongolian Fire Oil *

¼	pound bay scallops
½	small cucumber
¼	pound small cooked shrimp
¼	pound crab meat, flaked
1	cup cubed honeydew melon (½-inch cubes)
1	cup cubed cantaloupe (½-inch cubes)
4	cups shredded lettuce

* **House of Tsang Product**

1. Combine dressing ingredients in a small bowl and set aside.

2. Bring 2 cups water to a boil in a small saucepan. Add scallops; simmer for 2 minutes or until scallops turn opaque. Remove scallops; drain well and cool. Set aside.

3. Peel cucumber and cut in half lengthwise. Scoop out seeds. Thinly slice to make half moons.

4. Place scallops, shrimp, crab meat, honeydew melon, cantaloupe, lettuce, and cucumber in a large salad bowl. Add dressing; toss gently.

Comments: Small bay scallops, shrimp, and crab meat highlight this delicious seafood salad that also features honeydew melon and thin slices of cucumber. Crusty French bread and dry white wine are all you need to complete the menu.

Korean Donburi
(Stir-fried Chicken Teriyaki Over Rice)

Makes: 4 servings
Preparation time: 20 minutes

Cooking time: 6 minutes

¾   pound boneless chicken breasts

4   tablespoons Korean Teriyaki Sauce *

1   tablespoon Wok Oil *

½   onion, thinly sliced

½   cup thinly sliced mushrooms

1   zucchini, thinly sliced

4   eggs, lightly beaten

4   cups hot cooked rice

*   **House of Tsang Product**

1. Remove skin from chicken and cut meat into ½-inch cubes. Place in a bowl with 2 tablespoons of the teriyaki sauce; stir to coat. Set aside for 15 minutes.

2. Place a wok or large skillet over high heat until hot. Add wok oil, swirling to coat sides of pan. Add chicken; stir-fry for 2 minutes or until chicken turns opaque.

3. Add onion, mushrooms, and zucchini; stir-fry for 2 minutes. Stir in the remaining 2 tablespoons teriyaki sauce.

4. Reduce heat to medium-high. Add eggs and stir-fry for 2 minutes or until eggs form soft curds.

5. Divide rice among 4 bowls. Top each serving with one-fourth of the chicken-egg mixture.

Comments: Donburi makes a wonderful one-dish meal. Serve it with a tossed green salad and hot tea.

Tangy Bird
(Lemon Chicken)

Makes: 2 servings
Preparation time: 20 minutes

Cooking time: 4 minutes
Pictured on: Page 83

¾ pound boneless chicken breasts

MARINADE

1 tablespoon dry sherry

½ teaspoon salt

½ teaspoon Pure Sesame Seed Oil *

LEMON SAUCE

¼ cup fresh lemon juice

2 tablespoons brown sugar

2 tablespoons chicken broth

½ teaspoon Pure Sesame Seed Oil *

2 tablespoons Wok Oil *

3 green onions (including tops), cut into 1½-inch pieces

1 teaspoon grated lemon peel

1½ teaspoons cornstarch mixed with 1 tablespoon water

Lemon slices and cilantro (Chinese parsley) sprigs, for garnish

1. Remove skin from chicken and cut meat into thin slices. Combine marinade ingredients in a small bowl. Add chicken; stir to coat. Set aside for 15 minutes.

2. Combine lemon sauce ingredients in a small bowl and set aside.

3. Place a wok or large skillet over high heat until hot. Add wok oil, swirling to coat sides of pan. Add chicken; stir-fry for 2 minutes or until chicken turns opaque.

4. Add green onions, lemon peel, and lemon sauce ingredients; cook and stir for 1 minute. Add cornstarch solution and cook, stirring, until sauce boils and thickens slightly.

5. Transfer to a serving plate. Garnish with lemon slices and cilantro sprigs.

Comments: The tangy flavor of fresh lemon juice makes the difference in this sweet and sour sauce. Lemons yield the most juice when slightly warm or at room temperature. Place lemons on a dish in a microwave oven set on low for 2 minutes, or in a 300°F. oven for 5 minutes or until slightly warm.

*   **House of Tsang Product**

Enjoy our version of lemon chicken appropriately nicknamed Tangy Bird. Thin slices of marinated chicken breast are stir-fried with green onion, then presented in a tangy sauce made from fresh lemon juice, a touch of brown sugar, and grated lemon peel.

Flower Drums
(Five-spice Chicken Drummets)

Makes: 3 servings
Preparation time: 10 minutes

Cooking time: 13 minutes

SAUCE

⅓   cup chicken broth

1   tablespoon Ginger Flavored Soy Sauce *

1   tablespoon dry sherry

½   teaspoon sugar

¼   teaspoon Chinese five-spice

———————

14   chicken wing drummets

Salt

Pepper

2   tablespoons Wok Oil *

2   green onions (including tops), cut into 1-inch pieces

2   teaspoons cornstarch mixed with 4 teaspoons water

1. Combine sauce ingredients in a small bowl and set aside.

2. Lightly season chicken drummets with salt and pepper.

3. Place a wok or large skillet over high heat until hot. Add wok oil, swirling to coat sides of pan. Add drummets; cook, stirring, for 3 minutes or until brown. Add sauce ingredients; cover and simmer for 10 minutes or until drummets are cooked through. Stir in green onions. Add cornstarch solution and cook, stirring, until sauce boils and thickens slightly.

4. Transfer drummets to a serving platter and serve hot.

Comments: If you cannot find chicken drummets, use 7 whole chicken wings. Cut wings into sections, discarding the wing tips.

*   **House of Tsang Product**

Crescent Moons
(Cashew Chicken)

Makes: 4 servings
Preparation time: 20 minutes

Cooking time: 7 minutes

¾   pound boneless chicken breasts

1   tablespoon Mandarin Marinade *

1 ½   tablespoons Wok Oil *

2   stalks celery, thinly sliced

1   carrot, cut diagonally into ¼-inch slices

1   onion, thinly sliced

2   tablespoons chicken broth

2   tablespoons Classic Stir Fry Sauce *

½   cup roasted cashews

*   **House of Tsang Product**

1. Remove skin from chicken and cut meat into thin slices. Place in a bowl with marinade; stir to coat. Set aside for 15 minutes.

2. Place a wok or large skillet over high heat until hot. Add wok oil, swirling to coat sides of pan. Add chicken; stir-fry for 2 minutes or until chicken turns opaque. Add celery, carrot, onion, and chicken broth. Cover and cook for 3 minutes or until vegetables are crisp-tender.

3. Add stir fry sauce; cook, stirring, until heated through. Stir in cashews.

Comments: Very few recipes are easier to prepare than our stir-fried cashew chicken dish. Serve with your favorite steamed vegetable and a salad of seasonal greens.

Tsang Tempura—traditional Japanese tempura—is beautifully presented on a colorful lacquer tray. Medium-size shrimp, broccoli flowerets, asparagus, and slices of eggplant and sweet potato are served with dipping sauce and of course, chopsticks.

Tsang Tempura
(Deep-fried Seafood & Vegetables)

Makes: 4 servings
Preparation time: 20 minutes

Cooking time: 10 minutes
Pictured on: Page 86

DIPPING SAUCE

½   cup chicken broth

2   tablespoons Ginger Flavored Soy Sauce *

2   tablespoons dry sherry

½   teaspoon Hot Chili Sesame Oil *

---

2   eggs, lightly beaten

2   cups panko (Japanese bread crumbs)

   Vegetable oil for deep-frying

½   pound asparagus, trimmed

¼   pound green beans, trimmed

1   cup broccoli flowerets

1   Oriental eggplant, cut into ¼-inch thick slices

1   sweet potato, peeled and cut into ¼-inch thick slices

12   medium-size raw shrimp, shelled with tails left intact and deveined

1. Combine dipping sauce ingredients in a small bowl. Divide sauce into 4 small serving bowls and set aside.

2. Place eggs and panko in separate bowls and set aside.

3. Set wok in a ring stand and add vegetable oil to a depth of about 2 inches. Place over medium-high heat until oil reaches 350°F. on a deep-frying thermometer.

4. Dip vegetables in egg, a few pieces at a time, then roll in panko, shaking off excess. Add to oil, and deep-fry, turning occasionally, for 2 minutes or until golden brown. Lift out with a slotted spoon and drain on paper towels.

5. Cook the remaining vegetables and shrimp, 5 or 6 pieces at a time. Serve tempura as it is cooked or keep warm in a 200°F. oven while cooking remaining vegetables and shrimp.

6. Offer with dipping sauce at the table.

Comments: For best results, use a deep-frying thermometer to keep oil at a constant 350°F. Also, don't add too much food at one time as overloading the pan rapidly lowers the temperature of the oil.

*   **House of Tsang Product**

Guangzhou Scallops
(Scallops with Oriental Vegetables)

Makes: 4 servings
Preparation time: 25 minutes

Cooking time: 5 minutes

6   dried black mushrooms

¾   pound sea scallops

2   tablespoons dry sherry

SAUCE

2   tablespoons oyster sauce

2   tablespoons Ginger Flavored Soy Sauce *

1   cup chicken broth

1   teaspoon Hot Chili Sesame Oil *

⅛   teaspoon salt

---

2   tablespoons Wok Oil *

2   green onions (including tops), cut into 2-inch pieces

¾   cup sliced water chestnuts

¾   cup sliced bamboo shoots

¾   pound asparagus, ends trimmed, cut into 2-inch pieces

2   tablespoons cornstarch mixed with ¼ cup water

1. Soak mushrooms in enough warm water to cover for 20 minutes; drain. Cut off and discard stems; thinly slice caps and set aside.

2. Meanwhile, marinate scallops in sherry in a small bowl and set aside. Combine sauce ingredients in a small bowl and set aside.

3. Place a wok or large skillet over high heat until hot. Add 1 tablespoon of the wok oil, swirling to coat sides of pan. Add scallops; stir-fry for 2 minutes or until scallops turn opaque. Remove and set aside.

4. Add remaining 1 tablespoon wok oil to wok. Add green onions, water chestnuts, bamboo shoots, and asparagus; stir-fry for 2 minutes or until vegetables are crisp-tender.

5. Return scallops to wok. Add sauce mixture; bring to a boil. Add cornstarch solution and cook, stirring, until sauce boils and thickens slightly.

*   **House of Tsang Product**

Kung Pao Shrimp
(Shrimp with Four Flavors)

Makes: 4 servings
Preparation time: 25 minutes

Cooking time: 5 minutes

MARINADE

1   teaspoon Pure Sesame Seed Oil *

1   tablespoon dry sherry

¼   teaspoon salt

¾   pound medium-size raw shrimp, shelled and deveined

SAUCE

¼   cup chicken broth

2½   tablespoons Dark Soy Sauce *

2   tablespoons red wine vinegar

1½   teaspoons sugar

1   teaspoon Hot Chili Sesame Oil *

3   tablespoons Wok Oil *

6   dried small red chili peppers

½   onion, cut into 1-inch squares

¼   cup sliced bamboo shoots

1   green bell pepper, seeded and cut into 1-inch squares

2   teaspoons cornstarch mixed with 4 teaspoons water

*   **House of Tsang Product**

1. Combine marinade ingredients in a bowl. Add shrimp; stir to coat. Set aside for 15 minutes.

2. Combine sauce ingredients in a small bowl and set aside.

3. Place a wok or large skillet over high heat until hot. Add 2 tablespoons of the wok oil, swirling to coat sides of pan. Add shrimp and chili peppers; stir-fry for 2 minutes or until shrimp turn pink. Remove shrimp and chili peppers and set aside.

4. Add the remaining 1 tablespoon wok oil to wok. Add onion; cook for 30 seconds. Add bamboo shoots, bell pepper, and sauce mixture; cover and cook for 2 minutes or until bell pepper is crisp-tender.

5. Return shrimp and chili peppers to wok; cook and stir for 30 seconds. Add cornstarch solution and cook, stirring, until sauce boils and thickens slightly.

Comments: Salty, sweet, hot, and sour are the four flavors that enliven this popular dish from Szechuan.

Scarlet Warrior

(Chili-flavored Crab with Silver Noodles)

Makes: 4 servings
Preparation time: 6 minutes

Cooking time: 20 minutes
Pictured on: Page 91

2   ounces bean thread
    noodles

SAUCE

1½ cups chicken broth

1   tablespoon cornstarch

2   tablespoons Ginger
    Flavored Soy Sauce *

½   teaspoon sugar

⅛   teaspoon salt

⅛   teaspoon white pepper

———————————

1   tablespoon Wok Oil *

6   cloves garlic, peeled

½   cup chicken broth

1   cooked crab in shell,
    cleaned and cracked

4   thin slices fresh ginger

6   dried small red chili
    peppers

½   teaspoon ground
    turmeric

*   **House of Tsang Product**

1. Soak bean thread noodles in enough water to cover for 15 minutes. Drain, cut into 3-inch lengths, and set aside.

2. Combine sauce ingredients in a small bowl and set aside.

3. Place a 2-quart Chinese clay pot or 2-quart saucepan over medium heat until hot. Add wok oil, swirling to coat bottom of pan. Add garlic; cook for 1 minute. Add chicken broth, cover and simmer over low heat for 8 minutes or until garlic cloves are tender.

4. Add crab, ginger, chili peppers, turmeric, bean thread noodles, and sauce ingredients; mix well. Cover and simmer for 10 minutes or until bean thread noodles are tender.

Comments: You don't need a Chinese clay pot to cook this recipe, but the pot's rustic good looks allow you to cook and serve in the same pot. Heat the pot gradually and once hot, never put it on a wet surface. Sudden changes of temperature will cause the pot to crack.

Scarlet Warrior appears to be hiding, but this flavorful whole crab, seasoned with ginger, dried red chili peppers, turmeric and garlic, is actually cooked in the traditional Chinese clay pot along with bean thread noodles just as pictured.

Beijing Burgers
(Oriental Bacon Burgers)

Makes: 4 servings
Preparation time: 10 minutes

Cooking time: 10 minutes

1 pound lean ground beef
½ small onion, finely chopped
½ cup dry bread crumbs
1 egg, lightly beaten
3 tablespoons Hong Kong Barbecue Sauce *
½ teaspoon Hot Chili Sesame Oil *
8 strips bacon

* **House of Tsang Product**

1. Preheat broiler and adjust rack so meat will be 3 to 4 inches from heat.
2. Combine ground beef, onion, bread crumbs, egg, barbecue sauce, and chili sesame oil in a bowl; mix well. Divide mixture and shape into 4 patties.
3. Wrap 2 pieces of bacon crosswise around each patty as if tieing a package. Secure with wooden picks.
4. Place patties on a rack in a foil-lined broiling pan. Place under heat and broil for 5 minutes. Turn patties over and continue to broil for 5 more minutes for medium-rare. Remove wooden picks before serving.

Comments: Hong Kong Barbecue Sauce can also be used as a marinade or as a glazing sauce when roasting or barbecuing meat or poultry.

Asian Beef

(Beef & Asparagus in Black Bean Sauce)

Makes: 4 servings
Preparation time: 20 minutes   *Cooking time: 4 minutes*

¾   pound flank steak

MARINADE

1   tablespoon Dark Soy Sauce *

2   teaspoons dry sherry

1   teaspoon cornstarch

——————

1 ½ tablespoons fermented black beans

SAUCE

¼   cup chicken broth

2   tablespoons Ginger Flavored Soy Sauce *

1   teaspoon Hot Chili Sesame Oil *

1   teaspoon sugar

——————

¾   pound asparagus

2½ tablespoons Wok Oil *

½   teaspoon crushed red pepper

½   teaspoon minced garlic

½   teaspoon minced fresh ginger

1 ½ teaspoons cornstarch mixed with 1 tablespoon water

1. Slice beef across the grain into thin, slanting slices. Combine marinade ingredients in a bowl. Add beef; stir to coat. Set aside for 15 minutes.

2. Rinse black beans in cold water; drain and coarsely chop. Combine sauce ingredients in a small bowl. Cut off and discard tough ends of asparagus. Cut stalks diagonally into 2-inch pieces.

3. Place a wok or large skillet over high heat until hot. Add 2 tablespoons of the wok oil, swirling to coat sides of pan. Add beef; stir-fry for 1 ½ minutes or until barely pink. Remove beef from wok and set aside.

4. Add remaining ½ tablespoon wok oil to wok. Add black beans, red pepper, garlic, and ginger; cook until fragrant. Add asparagus; stir-fry for 2 minutes or until asparagus is crisp-tender.

5. Return beef to wok. Stir in sauce mixture; cook for 1 minute. Add cornstarch solution and cook, stirring, until sauces boils and thickens slightly.

Comments: Asparagus season is at its peak in March and April. It is available again from September through December, but in less supply. If asparagus is not available, substitute green beans, broccoli, or bok choy.

*   **House of Tsang Product**

Creative hosts love serving Mongolian Fire Pot because guests do all the work. The fire pot contains piping hot broth. Using small wire baskets, guests cook their choice of vegetables (cabbage, mushrooms, pea pods, bean curd) as well as pieces of chicken, beef, shrimp or fish balls right at the table.

Mongolian Fire Pot
(Family-style Meat & Vegetables)

Makes: 6 servings
Preparation time: 30 minutes

Cooking time: At the table
Pictured on: Page 94

10   dried black mushrooms

½   pound lean boneless sirloin or flank steak

½   pound raw shrimp

⅓   pound fish balls (purchased)

½   pound firm tofu, drained and cut into ¾-inch cubes

½   pound Chinese (napa) cabbage, cut into 2-inch pieces

½   pound bok choy

¼   pound snow peas, ends and strings removed

¼   pound fresh mushrooms, cut in half

DIPPING SAUCE #1

1   can (11 oz.) mandarin oranges, drained and pureed

⅓   cup Sweet & Sour Stir Fry Sauce *

2   teaspoons grated lemon peel

DIPPING SAUCE #2

½   cup coconut milk

½   cup salted peanuts, chopped

1   tablespoon Singapore Curry Oil *

⅛   teaspoon crushed red pepper

1. Soak black mushrooms in enough warm water to cover for 20 minutes; drain. Cut off and discard stems and set caps aside.

2. Meanwhile, thinly slice beef across the grain. Shell and devein shrimp, if desired, or leave shells on shrimp as illustrated on opposite page.

3. Arrange beef, shrimp, fish balls, tofu, Chinese cabbage, bok choy, snow peas, fresh mushrooms, and black mushrooms on a platter or in a flat basket.

4. Prepare dipping sauces; pour into small individual bowls.

5. Bring chicken broth to a boil in a large saucepan. At the table, pour broth into an Oriental hot pot, electric wok, or electric frying pan. Let each guest cook small quantities of each ingredient briefly in broth, then lift out and dip into one of the sauces. Ladle broth into bowls for sipping after all the food is cooked.

Comments: Guests don't mind cooking their own dinner when they participate in a traditional Mongolian Fire Pot supper. A charcoal-fired Oriental hot pot is available in Oriental hardware stores. Be sure to use one made of metal suitable for cooking, such as brass or stainless steel. Some are designed purely for ornamental use. To fire a hot pot, fill the moat with hot cooking broth, then half fill the chimney with glowing charcoal. Be sure to put broth in the moat before adding coals, otherwise the heat of the charcoal may

(Continued)

DIPPING SAUCE #3

¼ cup chicken broth

2 tablespoons Ginger
   Flavored Soy Sauce *

1 green onion (including
   top), thinly sliced

8 cups chicken broth

* **House of Tsang Product**

melt the pot's solder. Once filled with charcoal, the bottom of the pot becomes very hot, so protect your table well.

Fish balls, made from ground white fish fillets, make a delicious addition to Mongolian Fire Pot. They are available fresh or frozen in Chinese markets, and because they are pre-cooked, they need only a few minutes of simmering in the broth to heat through.

Pagoda Pork Chops
(Spicy Pork Chops with Onion)

Makes: 4 servings
Preparation time: 10 minutes

Cooking time: 20 minutes

SAUCE

¼ cup chicken broth

2 tablespoons Hoisin
   Sauce *

1 tablespoon dry sherry

1 teaspoon Mongolian
   Fire Oil *

2 teaspoons Ginger
   Flavored Soy Sauce *

1½ tablespoons Wok Oil *

4 pork chops, each about
   ¾-inch thick

½ onion, thinly sliced

* **House of Tsang Product**

1. Combine sauce ingredients in a small bowl and set aside.

2. Place a large skillet over medium heat until hot. Add wok oil, swirling to coat bottom of pan.

3. Add pork chops and cook over medium heat for 3 minutes on each side or until brown.

4. Add onion and sauce mixture; cook over low heat for 15 minutes or until pork is cooked through and sauce is reduced to a thick glaze.

Comments: Here's a tasty yet unusual way to serve pork chops. Steamed seasonal vegetables or a salad of fresh greens and pasta are great accompaniments.

Chinese Sausage Grill

(Grilled Pork Sausage & Vegetables)

Makes: 4 servings
Preparation time: 15 minutes

Cooking time: 15 minutes

MARINADE

¼ cup ketchup

2 tablespoons cider vinegar

1 tablespoon Hot Chili Sesame Oil *

2 tablespoons Ginger Flavored Soy Sauce *

1 teaspoon minced garlic

1 teaspoon minced fresh ginger

————————

1 pound link pork sausages

15 mushrooms, stems trimmed

2 red or green bell peppers, cut in half lengthwise, seeded

2 zucchini, cut in half lengthwise

* **House of Tsang Product**

1. Combine marinade ingredients in a large bowl; whisk until evenly blended. Add sausages, mushrooms, bell peppers, and zucchini; stir to coat. Set aside for 15 minutes.

2. Preheat broiler and adjust rack so meat and vegetables will be 3 to 4 inches from heat.

3. Thread mushrooms on 3 skewers. Place mushrooms, sausages, bell peppers, and zucchini on a rack in a foil-lined broiling pan. Place under heat and broil, turning occasionally and brushing with marinade, for 15 minutes or until sausages are cooked through and vegetables are tender. (You may also grill the sausages and vegetables on a barbecue grill about 4 inches above a solid bed of low-glowing coals.)

4. Remove mushrooms from skewers. Immediately slice sausages and vegetables into 1-inch pieces and toss mixture together. Serve hot.

Comments: One-third cup Hong Kong Barbecue Sauce with 1 tablespoon Hot Chili Sesame Oil may be substituted for marinade ingredients.

Sweet & Sour Pork

(Classic Sweet & Sour Pork)

Makes: 4 servings
Preparation time: 10 minutes

Cooking time: 20 minutes
Pictured on: Page 99

1   pound boneless lean
    pork

MARINADE

1   tablespoon Dark Soy
    Sauce *

1   tablespoon dry sherry

1   egg yolk

1   tablespoon cornstarch

1   can (20 oz.) pineapple
    chunks, packed in un-
    sweetened juice

SAUCE

½   cup cider vinegar

⅓   cup ketchup

3   tablespoons maraschino
    cherry juice (optional)

⅓   cup packed brown sugar

½   teaspoon Pure Sesame
    Seed Oil *

COATING

¼   cup all-purpose flour

¼   cup cornstarch

    Vegetable oil

⅓   cup maraschino cherries

1   green bell pepper,
    seeded and cut into
    1-inch squares

1. Cut pork into ¾-inch cubes. Combine marinade ingredients in a bowl. Add pork; stir to coat. Set aside for 5 minutes.

2. Drain pineapple, reserving ⅓ cup juice. Set pineapple aside. Combine reserved juice with sauce ingredients in a bowl and set aside. Combine flour and cornstarch in another bowl.

3. Remove pork from marinade. Coat pork with flour-cornstarch mixture, shaking off excess.

4. Set wok in a ring stand and add vegetable oil to a depth of about 2 inches. Place over medium-high heat until oil reaches 360°F. on a deep-frying thermometer. Add pork, a few pieces at a time, and deep-fry for 6 to 8 minutes or until browned and cooked through. Lift out with a slotted spoon and drain on paper towels. Keep warm in a 200°F. oven while cooking remaining pork.

5. Place a clean wok over medium-high heat until hot. Add 1 teaspoon vegetable oil, swirling to coat sides of pan. Add sauce mixture, cherries, bell pepper, and pineapple. Stir-fry for 2 minutes or until bell pepper is crisp-tender.

6. Add pork cubes to sauce and cook, stirring, for 30 seconds or until heated through.

Comments: A classic dish that gets high marks from kids and grownups alike. When time is at a premium, you can substitute our own Sweet & Sour Sauce for the sauce recipe above.

*Guaranteed to please friends and family alike, colorful Sweet &
Sour Pork combines cubes of marinated pork, stir-fried with bell
pepper that is served in a sweet and sour sauce containing
pineapple bits and maraschino cherries.*

Empress-style Pears

(Pears with Candied Ginger Sauce)

Makes: 4 servings
Preparation time: 15 minutes

Cooking time: 10 minutes

4   firm, medium pears
     (Bartlett or Anjou)

3   tablespoons orange
     marmalade

SAUCE

½   cup packed brown sugar

¼   cup butter or margarine

2   tablespoons chopped
     candied ginger

     Pinch of Chinese five-
     spice

     Whipped cream
     (optional)

     Additional candied
     ginger, cut into very
     thin slivers

1. Slice about 1 inch off from the top of each pear. Save the tops as "lids." Using a melon baller, carefully scoop out cores, leaving about 1 inch of flesh at bottom of each pear.

2. Spoon about 2 teaspoons marmalade into each pear; cover with "lids." Stand pears, lid side up, in a heat-proof dish. Place dish in steamer or on a rack in a wok. Cover and steam over boiling water for 10 minutes or until tender when pierced with a fork.

3. While pears are steaming, combine sauce ingredients in a small saucepan. Cook, stirring, over medium heat until brown sugar and butter melt and sauce is evenly blended.

4. To serve, spoon a little sauce into each dessert bowl. Stand a pear in each bowl, then drizzle a little remaining sauce over each. Garnish with a small dollop of whipped cream and a few slivers of candied ginger.

Comments: Candied ginger is the special flavoring in this elegant fruit dessert. For a festive presentation, place each bowl on a doily-lined glass plate and decorate with a small flower.

Rainbow Fruit Medley
(Brandied Kiwi & Oranges)

Makes: 4 servings
Preparation time: 25 minutes

Cooking time: 3 minutes

SYRUP

½   cup water

¼   cup sugar

4   thin slices fresh ginger

1   piece (about 3 inches)
    Chinese cinnamon bark
    or cinnamon stick

2   tablespoons Sweet &
    Sour Stir Fry Sauce *

―――――――――

4   oranges

3   kiwi fruit

2   tablespoons brandy

Mint sprigs, for garnish

*   **House of Tsang Product**

1. Combine syrup ingredients in a small saucepan; bring to a boil and cook for 3 minutes. Remove and discard ginger slices and cinnamon bark. Chill while preparing remaining ingredients.

2. Peel and thinly slice oranges and kiwi fruit. Combine fruit with brandy in a bowl. Let stand for 15 minutes, stirring occasionally. Pour off brandy and add it to the ginger syrup.

3. Spoon fruit into 4 dessert bowls. Dividing it equally, pour syrup over each serving. Garnish with mint sprigs.

Comments: The lively flavor of ginger enhances any dish. The rhizome of a tropical plant, ginger is sold fresh, in crystallized cubes or slices, or dried and ground. In Chinese cooking, do not substitute ground ginger for the fresh root.

Savory Sensations
Recipes for Less than 1 hour

For once you're not rushing off—no evening meetings, no one to meet downtown, just the chance to relax and enjoy a wonderful meal.

So, take a moment to glance over some of the recipes in the Savory Sensations chapter. All of them are special and all take less than an hour to prepare.

Those few extra minutes allow time for stewing and braising meat, such as in Toishan Veal (page 121), for practicing special cutting techniques for vegetables, and for preparing speciality dishes like Mu Shu Pork (page 119) or Sisters From The Sea (page 114).

An hour is also plenty of time to prepare a sensational meal that combines something steamed, something stir-fried, and something baked. You are the chef tonight, so let your imagination help you create your own savory sensations.

Dragon's Broth
(Hot & Sour Soup)

Makes: 8 servings
Preparation time: 35 minutes

Cooking time: 10 minutes

2   dried wood ears (tree mushrooms)

¼   pound boneless chicken breast

MARINADE

1   teaspoon cornstarch

½   teaspoon sugar

1   tablespoon Ginger Flavored Soy Sauce *

2   teaspoons dry sherry

---

6   cups chicken broth

1   can (4 oz.) sliced button mushrooms, drained

½   cup frozen peas, thawed

8   ounces regular or firm tofu, drained and cut into ½-inch cubes

⅓   cup white wine vinegar

1   tablespoon Dark Soy Sauce *

¾   teaspoon white pepper

1   teaspoon Hot Chili Sesame Oil*

½   teaspoon salt

⅓   cup cornstarch mixed with ⅓ cup water

1   egg white, lightly beaten

1   green onion (including top), thinly sliced, for garnish

1. Soak wood ears in enough warm water to cover for 30 minutes; drain. Thinly slice wood ears. (You should have about ½ cup.) Set aside.

2. Meanwhile, remove skin from chicken and cut meat into thin slices. Combine marinade ingredients in a small bowl. Add chicken; stir to coat. Set aside for 15 minutes.

3. Bring chicken broth to a boil in a large saucepan. Add chicken, wood ears, and mushrooms. Cook over medium-high heat, stirring occasionally, for 3 minutes.

4. Add peas, tofu, wine vinegar, soy sauce, white pepper, chili sesame oil, and salt. Bring to a boil. Add cornstarch solution and cook, stirring constantly, until soup boils and thickens slightly.

5. Remove soup from heat and slowly drizzle in egg white, stirring constantly. Serve soup in individual bowls garnished with a sprinkling of green onion.

Comments: What makes Hot & Sour Soup hot? It's the white pepper, so you can always increase or decrease the amount according to your liking.

*   **House of Tsang Product**

Tsang Spring Rolls
(Chinese Sausage & Vegetables in Filo)

Makes: 14 rolls
Preparation time: 40 minutes   *Cooking time: 10 minutes*

FILLING

2   Chinese sausages (lop cheong), cut into matchstick pieces

1   carrot, shredded

2   cups shredded cabbage

1   cup shredded bamboo shoots

2   green onions (including tops), cut into 2-inch slivers

1   tablespoon dry sherry

2   tablespoons oyster sauce

2   teaspoons Hot Chili Sesame Oil *

¼   teaspoon white pepper

---

7   sheets filo dough

¼   cup melted butter

1   tablespoon sesame seeds

*   **House of Tsang Product**

1. Place a wok or large skillet over high heat until hot. Add Chinese sausages; cook for 1 minute. Add carrot, cabbage, and bamboo shoots; cook for 3 minutes or until vegetables are crisp-tender. Stir in green onions and sherry; cook for 30 seconds. Add oyster sauce, chili sesame oil, and white pepper; cook, stirring, for 1 minute or until there is no liquid in bottom of pan. Remove from heat and let filling cool to room temperature.

2. Carefully stack 7 sheets of filo together on the work surface. With scissors or a sharp knife, cut through the stack, crosswise into 4 sections each about 4 inches x 12 inches. (28 strips total.) (Cover with a dry kitchen towel to prevent drying.)

3. To make each spring roll, lightly brush butter over one strip. Cover with a second strip of filo and lightly brush with butter. Spoon about 3 tablespoons filling across one short end of filo, leaving a 1-inch border along edges. Roll edge of filo over to enclose filling, fold in either side, and continue to roll. Dampen top edge of filo with water and press gently to seal.

4. Place rolls, seam side down, in an ungreased shallow rimmed baking pan. Brush tops with butter and sprinkle with sesame seeds. (If you wish you may cover and refrigerate for up to 8 hours before cooking.)

5. Bake rolls in a 375°F. oven, uncovered, for 15 minutes or until puffed and golden brown. Serve warm.

Chinese Flap Jacks

(Green Onion Pancakes)

Makes: 8 pancakes
Preparation time: 10 minutes

Cooking time: 25 minutes

1 ½ cups all-purpose flour

3   eggs, lightly beaten

2   green onions (including tops), thinly sliced

1   teaspoon sugar

2   teaspoons Hot Chili Sesame Oil *

¾   teaspoon salt

¾   cup water

2   tablespoons Wok Oil *

*   **House of Tsang Product**

1. Combine flour, eggs, green onions, sugar, chili sesame oil, and salt in a bowl. Add water; stir until smooth.

2. Place a large frying pan or griddle with a nonstick finish over medium-high heat. Grease lightly with wok oil. Cooking 3 pancakes at a time, pour batter, about ⅓ cup for each pancake, onto hot pan. Spread batter out to make a 5-inch circle. Cook for 5 minutes or until golden. Turn over and cook for 2 minutes more or until golden.

3. Remove from pan; keep warm in a 200°F. oven while cooking remaining pancakes.

Comments: Green onion pancakes are wonderful anytime. Serve them as a snack or as a bread substitute during a meal. They can be made in advance and then reheated (I often use a microwave oven) just before serving.

Potstickers
(Mandarin-style Meat Dumplings)

Makes: 28 potstickers
Preparation time: 40 minutes

Cooking time: 18 minutes
Pictured on : Page 107

DOUGH

3 cups all-purpose flour

1⅓ cups boiling water

FILLING

5 dried black mushrooms

½ pound ground veal

2 green onions (including tops), finely chopped

1¼ cups finely shredded cabbage

1 tablespoon Dark Soy Sauce *

1 tablespoon dry sherry

1 tablespoon cornstarch

1 teaspoon Hot Chili Sesame Oil *

1 teaspoon minced fresh ginger

½ teaspoon sugar

2 tablespoons vegetable oil

⅔ cup chicken broth

CONDIMENTS

Dark Soy Sauce *

Rice vinegar

Mongolian Fire Oil *

* **House of Tsang Product**

1. Measure flour into a large bowl. Mix in boiling water, stirring with a fork until dough is evenly moistened. Cover and let rest for 30 minutes.

2. Meanwhile, soak mushrooms in enough warm water to cover for 30 minutes; drain. Cut off and discard stems; finely chop caps. Combine mushrooms with remaining filling ingredients in a medium bowl; mix well.

3. On a lightly floured surface, knead dough for about 5 minutes or until smooth and elastic. Divide dough in half. Roll each half into a 14-inch long cylinder. Cut each cylinder crosswise into 1-inch thick pieces; shape each piece into a ball.

4. To shape each potsticker, flatten 1 ball of dough with a rolling pin to make a 3-inch circle; keep remaining dough covered to prevent drying. Place 1 heaping teaspoon of filling in center of circle. Lightly moisten edges of circle with water. Fold circle in half over filling to form a semi-circle. Starting at one end, pinch curved edges together; make 4 to 6 pleats along the edge facing you, pressing edges to seal securely. Set potsticker down firmly, seam side up. Cover filled potsticker with a damp cloth while shaping remaining potstickers.

5. Place a wide frying pan with a nonstick finish over medium-high heat until hot. Add 1 tablespoon of the vegetable oil, swirling to coat sides of pan. Set half the potstickers, seam side up, without crowding, in pan. Cook for 2 to 2½ minutes or until bottoms are golden. Drain excess oil and reduce

(Continued)

Perfect as an appetizer or just for a snack, these meat-filled dumplings are pan-fried to a golden brown and then braised. Serve Potstickers with your choice of dipping sauce, or with our favorite, Mongolian Fire Oil combined with rice vinegar.

heat to medium-low. Pour in ⅓ cup of chicken broth; cover and cook for 5 to 6 minutes or until liquid evaporates. Transfer potstickers to a serving platter and keep warm in a 200°F. oven. Cook remaining potstickers with remaining oil and broth.

6. Serve potstickers with your choice of condiments.

———

Bombay Madness
(Vegetarian Curried Rice)

Makes: 4 to 6 servings
Preparation time: 35 minutes

Cooking time: 5 minutes

6	dried black mushrooms
2	tablespoons Wok Oil *
½	cup thinly sliced fresh mushrooms
½	red bell pepper, seeded and cut into thin strips
4	cups cooked long-grain rice
2	tablespoons water
1	tablespoon Singapore Curry Oil *
1	teaspoon Hot Chili Sesame Oil *
¾	teaspoon salt
¼	teaspoon sugar
⅓	cup frozen peas, thawed
¼	cup pineapple tidbits, drained
2	green onions (including tops), thinly sliced

1. Soak black mushrooms in enough warm water to cover for 30 minutes; drain. Cut off and discard stems; thinly slice caps.

2. Place a wok or large skillet over high heat until hot. Add wok oil, swirling to coat sides of pan.

3. Add fresh mushrooms, black mushrooms, and bell pepper; cook for 1 minute.

4. Stir in rice, breaking up clumps with a spoon. Add water, curry oil, chili sesame oil, salt, and sugar; stir-fry for 2 minutes.

5. Stir in peas, pineapple, and green onions; cook until heated through.

Comments: Black mushrooms, peas, strips of bell pepper, and pineapple combine in this hot curry-flavored rice side dish. Serve it with any grilled meat or simply prepared seafood entree.

* **House of Tsang Product**

Savory Chicken Wings
(Broiled Honey-Ginger Chicken Wings)

Makes: 24 appetizers
Preparation time: 30 minutes

Cooking time: 10 minutes

12 chicken wings
    (about 2 lbs.)

MARINADE

3   tablespoons Dark Soy
    Sauce *

3   tablespoons honey

2   tablespoons cider
    vinegar or lemon juice

1   tablespoon dry sherry

2   teaspoons minced garlic

2   teaspoons minced fresh
    ginger

1   teaspoon Pure Sesame
    Seed Oil *

¼   teaspoon crushed red
    pepper

* **House of Tsang Product**

1. Cut off and discard chicken wing tips. Cut remaining part of wings in half at joints to make 24 pieces.

2. Combine marinade ingredients in a large bowl. Add chicken; stir to coat. Set aside for 30 minutes.

3. Preheat broiler and adjust rack so that chicken will be 3 to 4 inches from heat.

4. Lift chicken, reserving marinade, and place on a rack in a foil-lined broiling pan. Broil, basting occasionally with reserved marinade, for 5 minutes on each side or until juices run clear when chicken is pierced with a knife.

5. Transfer to a platter and serve hot.

Comments: Serve these honey and ginger-flavored chicken appetizers at your next party. Or, for a simple dinner for two, offer chicken accompanied by steamed rice and a hearty vegetable such as artichokes or sugar or snap peas.

Resting on a bed of baby bok choy leaves, From The Garden is a trio of savory mushrooms—straw, black and button varieties—napped with a soy, oyster-flavored sauce. Chinese believe that to serve them is to offer your guests wealth and prosperity.

From The Garden
(Braised Straw, Button & Black Mushrooms)

Makes: 4 servings
Preparation time: 30 minutes

Cooking time: 25 minutes
Pictured on: Page 110

16   dried black mushrooms

1¼ cups chicken broth

12   baby bok choy leaves,
     for garnish

1   can (4 oz.) whole button
     mushrooms, rinsed and
     drained

1   can (15 oz.) straw mush-
     rooms, rinsed and
     drained

3   tablespoons Dark Soy
     Sauce *

2   tablespoons oyster sauce

1½ tablespoons cornstarch
     mixed with 3 table-
     spoons water

*   **House of Tsang Product**

1. Soak black mushrooms in enough warm water to cover for 30 minutes; drain. Cut off and discard stems.

2. Place black mushrooms and chicken broth in a medium saucepan. Bring to a boil over high heat. Cover, reduce heat, and simmer for 20 minutes or until mushrooms are tender.

3. While simmering mushrooms, blanch bok choy leaves in boiling water for 30 seconds. Refresh under cold running water; drain well. Line a platter with the bok choy leaves. Set aside.

4. When black mushrooms are tender, add button and straw mushrooms, soy sauce, and oyster sauce; simmer for 5 minutes.

5. Add cornstarch solution and cook, stirring, until sauce boils and thickens slightly.

6. Spoon mushrooms on top of bok choy leaves and serve hot.

Comments: Traditionally, black mushrooms are served at festive occasions, not only for flavor, but for symbolic meaning. The round shapes of black mushrooms symbolize coins. To serve them is to offer your guests wealth and prosperity.

Peking Chicken Skewers

(Grilled Bacon & Chicken Kebabs)

Makes: 4 to 6 servings
Preparation time: 40 minutes

Cooking time: 14 minutes

SAUCE

⅓ cup ketchup

2 tablespoons Ginger Flavored Soy Sauce *

1 tablespoon Worcestershire sauce

2 teaspoons brown sugar

1 teaspoon Hot Chili Sesame Oil *

1¼ pounds boneless chicken breasts

12 strips bacon

2 medium zucchini, cut diagonally into ½-inch thick slices

18 large mushrooms

* **House of Tsang Product**

1. Prepare grill for barbecuing.

2. Soak six 12-inch bamboo skewers in water while preparing kebabs.

3. Combine sauce ingredients in a bowl. Remove skin from chicken and cut meat into 2-inch cubes. Add chicken to sauce; stir to coat. Set aside for 30 minutes.

4. Lift chicken from sauce, reserving sauce. To thread each skewer, pierce one end of a bacon strip with a skewer. Then thread on a piece of chicken, a piece of zucchini, and a mushroom. Weave bacon around chicken, zucchini, and mushroom (s-shape) and thread onto skewer. Repeat, threading bacon, chicken, zucchini, and mushroom; use 2 strips of bacon for each skewer. Brush filled skewers with reserved sauce.

5. Place on prepared barbecue grill 4 inches above a solid bed of low-glowing coals. Cook, turning often and brushing with reserved sauce, for 12 to 14 minutes or until bacon is crisp and chicken is opaque.

Comments: You may also broil kebabs in the oven. Place kebabs on a rack in a foil-lined broiling pan. Place 3 to 4 inches from heat and broil, basting and turning frequently.

Yellow Sea Dragon

(Oriental Steamed Whole Fish)

Makes: 4 servings
Preparation time: 35 minutes

Cooking time: 20 minutes

4	dried black mushrooms
1	whole rock cod (about 2 lbs.) cleaned and scaled (or 1½ pounds firm white fish fillets, each about ¾-inch thick)
4	quarter-size slices fresh ginger
½	cup chicken broth
¼	cup sliced water chestnuts
1	green onion (including top), cut into 1½-inch slivers
1	tablespoon Ginger Flavored Soy Sauce *
1	teaspoon Pure Sesame Seed Oil *
½	teaspoon sugar
⅛	teaspoon white pepper
2	teaspoons cornstarch mixed with 4 teaspoons water
¼	cup chopped roasted cashews

Cilantro sprigs (Chinese parsley), for garnish

* **House of Tsang Product**

1. Soak mushrooms in enough warm water to cover for 30 minutes; drain. Cut off and discard stems; thinly slice caps. Set aside.

2. On each side of fish, make 3 or 4 diagonal slices about 1 inch apart. (If using fillets, do not slash) Place fish on a heatproof dish that will fit in a steamer or on a rack in a wok. Place ginger and mushroom slices on fish.

3. Place dish in a steamer or on a rack in a wok. Cover and steam over boiling water for 15 minutes (8 minutes for fillets) or until fish turns opaque and just begins to flake.

4. Remove dish from steamer. With a slotted spatula, lift and transfer fish to a serving platter, reserving cooking juices for sauce. Cover loosely with foil to keep warm.

5. Pour cooking juices and mushrooms into a small saucepan; discard ginger. Add chicken broth, water chestnuts, green onion, soy sauce, sesame oil, sugar, and white pepper. Bring to a boil. Add cornstarch solution and cook, stirring, until sauce boils again and thickens slightly.

6. Pour sauce over fish. Sprinkle the top with cashews and garnish with cilantro sprigs.

Comments: It's easy to see where the name "sea dragon" comes from once you've prepared a steamed whole fish — especially a whole fish that looks like rock cod! But don't let the appearance deceive you. Our friendly dragon, seasoned with slices of ginger, black mushrooms, water chestnuts, and slivers of green onion, is wonderful.

Sisters From The Sea
(Seafood with Pan-fried Noodles)

Makes: 6 servings
Preparation time: 20 minutes

Cooking time: 25 minutes
Pictured on: Page 115

MARINADE

1   teaspoon cornstarch

1   tablespoon dry sherry

¼   teaspoon salt

½   pound medium-size raw shrimp, shelled and deveined

½   pound sea scallops

SWEET AND SOUR SAUCE

½   cup pineapple juice

½   cup chicken broth

½   cup cider vinegar

¼   cup ketchup

¼   cup granulated sugar

2   tablespoons brown sugar

1   tablespoon Ginger Flavored Soy Sauce *

NOODLES

1   pound Chinese noodles

2   teaspoons Pure Sesame Seed Oil *

1   tablespoon Ginger Flavored Soy Sauce *

---

3   tablespoons Wok Oil*

2   teaspoons minced garlic

¼   teaspoon white pepper

1   (each) red, green, and yellow bell pepper, cut into matchstick pieces

1. Combine marinade ingredients in a bowl. Add shrimp and scallops; stir to coat. Set aside for 15 minutes.

2. Combine sweet and sour sauce ingredients in a small bowl; set aside.

3. Cook noodles according to package directions until tender but firm to the bite; drain. Toss noodles with sesame oil and soy sauce.

4. Place a wide frying pan with a nonstick finish over medium heat until hot. Add 1½ teaspoons of the wok oil, swirling to coat bottom of pan. Add half of the noodles, spreading evenly over bottom of pan. Cook noodles for 4 minutes, turn over and cook for 4 minutes more, or until golden brown. Place noodle pancake on a large heatproof serving platter; keep warm in a 200°F. oven while cooking remaining noodle pancake in 1½ more teaspoons of the wok oil. Place second pancake on a large serving platter and keep warm in oven.

5. Place a wok or large skillet over high heat until hot. Add 1 tablespoon of the wok oil, swirling to coat sides of pan. Add garlic; cook stirring until fragrant. Add shrimp, scallops, and white pepper; stir-fry for 2 minutes or until shrimp turn pink. Remove and set aside.

6. Add the remaining 1 tablespoon wok oil, swirling to coat sides of pan. Add bell peppers; stir-fry for 1 minute. Add sweet and sour sauce. Cook for 3 or 4 minutes or until bell peppers are crisp-tender. Add cornstarch solution; cook, stirring, until sauce boils and thickens slightly.

(Continued)

Dazzle guests at your next party by offering Sisters From The Sea. Tender shrimp, fresh sea scallops, julienne strips of red, green and yellow pepper, garlic and green onion are cooked in a sweet and sour sauce, then served over pan-fried Chinese noodles.

2	tablespoons cornstarch mixed with ¼ cup water
3	green onions (including tops), cut into ½-inch diagonal slices
1	teaspoon Hot Chili Sesame Oil *

*   **House of Tsang Product**

7. Return shrimp and scallops to pan. Stir in green onions. Sprinkle with chili sesame oil.

8. Divide mixture and spoon over noodle pancakes to serve.

Comments: You'll enjoy serving seafood over pan-fried noodles for two reasons: the presentation is spectacular and the flavor outstanding. I know it will become one of your favorites, too.

Seoul Bones
(Oven-baked Short Ribs)

Makes: 4 servings
Preparation time: 20 minutes

Cooking time: 40 minutes

MARINADE

¼	cup Ginger Flavored Soy Sauce *
2	tablespoons red wine vinegar
2	teaspoons dry mustard
1	teaspoon sugar

2½ pounds beef short ribs

*   **House of Tsang Product**

1. Combine marinade ingredients in a large bowl. Add short ribs; stir to coat. Set aside for 15 minutes, turning occasionally.

2. Lift short ribs from marinade, reserving marinade. Place on a rack in a foil-lined baking pan. Bake ribs in a 375°F. oven, basting occasionally with reserved marinade, for 40 minutes for medium-rare or until done to your liking.

3. Transfer short ribs to a platter and serve hot.

Comments: When time is at a premium or when you're missing an ingredient or two, substitute ½ cup House of Tsang Korean Teriyaki Sauce for the marinade ingredients. Offer freshly-cooked Chinese noodles seasoned with butter and a pinch of black sesame seeds plus a salad of fresh greens to accompany Seoul Bones.

Time-to-spare Ribs
(Braised Orange-flavored Ribs)

Makes: 4 servings
Preparation time: 20 minutes

Cooking time: 35 minutes

2   pounds pork spareribs

MARINADE

2   tablespoons Ginger
    Flavored Soy Sauce *

2   tablespoons dry sherry

BRAISING LIQUID

½   cup orange juice

¼   cup chicken broth

2   tablespoons rice vinegar

2   tablespoons Ginger
    Flavored Soy Sauce *

2   tablespoons brown sugar

1   tablespoon cornstarch

2   teaspoons grated orange
    peel

1   teaspoon minced garlic

———

2   tablespoons Wok Oil *

* **House of Tsang Product**

1. Trim excess fat from spareribs; cut between the bones to make individual pieces.

2. Combine marinade ingredients in a large bowl. Add spareribs; stir to coat. Set aside for 20 minutes.

3. Combine braising liquid ingredients in a bowl and set aside.

4. Place a wok or large skillet over high heat until hot. Add wok oil, swirling to coat sides of pan. Add spareribs; stir-fry for 4 minutes or until lightly brown. Drain excess oil. Add braising liquid; cover and simmer for 30 minutes or until ribs are tender when pierced.

5. Transfer spareribs to a serving platter and serve hot.

Comments: Pork ribs first marinate in Ginger Flavored Soy Sauce and then are braised in an orange-flavored sauce that has just a hint of sweetness. Serve with hot cooked rice and seasonal vegetables.

Lean pork, bamboo shoots, bean sprouts, shredded cabbage, green onion, and two kinds of exotic Oriental ingredients make a tempting combination in this traditional dish. Enjoy Mu Shu Pork wrapped in steamed Mandarin Pancakes that have been first brushed with hoisin sauce.

Mu Shu Pork

(Pancakes with Stir-fried Pork & Vegetables)

Makes: 8 servings
Preparation time: 45 minutes

Cooking time: 12 minutes
Pictured on: Page 118

4   dried wood ears (tree mushrooms)

½   cup dried tiger lily buds

¾   pound boneless lean pork

MARINADE

1   tablespoon Dark Soy Sauce *

1   tablespoon dry sherry

1   teaspoon cornstarch

2   tablespoons Wok Oil *

3   eggs, lightly beaten

16   Mandarin Pancakes (page 140 or purchased)

1   cup sliced bamboo shoots, cut into matchstick pieces

3   cups shredded cabbage

¼   cup chicken broth

3   tablespoons Ginger Flavored Soy Sauce *

2   cups bean sprouts

1   teaspoon Hot Chili Sesame Oil *

¼   teaspoon white pepper

2   green onions (including tops), cut into 2-inch slivers

1   tablespoon cornstarch mixed with 2 tablespoons water

½   cup Hoisin Sauce *

1. In separate bowls, soak wood ears and lily buds in enough warm water to cover for 30 minutes; drain. Thinly slice wood ears and set aside. Cut off and discard hard tips of lily buds and set aside.

2. Meanwhile, cut pork into matchstick pieces. Combine marinade ingredients in a small bowl. Add pork; stir to coat. Set aside for 15 minutes.

3. Place a wide frying pan with a nonstick finish over medium-high heat until hot. Add 1 teaspoon wok oil, swirling to coat sides of pan. Pour in half the eggs. Cook just until eggs are set and feel dry on top. Remove from pan and cook remaining eggs. Cool; cut omelet into 3-inch long strips; set aside.

4. Separate pancakes and then fold in half. Arrange inside a cloth napkin. Place napkin in a bamboo steamer and steam over boiling water for 4 or 5 minutes. Turn off heat and keep warm in steamer while cooking meat mixture.

5. Place a wok or large skillet over high heat until hot. Add remaining wok oil, swirling to coat sides of pan. Add pork; stir-fry for 2 minutes or until lightly browned. Add wood ears, lily buds, bamboo shoots, cabbage, and chicken broth. Cook and toss for 2 minutes.

6. Stir in soy sauce, bean sprouts, chili sesame oil, white pepper, and green onions; cook for 1 minute. Add cornstarch solution and cook, stirring, until sauce boils and thickens slightly. Place in a serving platter and garnish with omelet strips.

(Continued)

7. Place hoisin sauce and pancakes on the table alongside pork. Have guests spread a small amount of hoisin sauce in each pancake, then place about 3 tablespoons of meat-vegetable mixture down the center of pancake. Wrap up pancake like a burrito and eat out of hand.

———

Mongolian Lamb
(Lamb & Vegetable Stir-fry)

Makes: 4 servings
Preparation time: 30 minutes

Cooking time: 6 minutes

1   pound boneless lean lamb (leg or shoulder)

8   cups assorted vegetables, such as Oriental egg-plant, carrot, onion, bell pepper, mushrooms, bean sprouts, Chinese (napa) cabbage, and green onions

2½ tablespoons Wok Oil *

¾   cup Korean Teriyaki Sauce *

Hot Chili Sesame Oil *

* **House of Tsang Product**

1. Thinly slice lamb across the grain, then cut into strips, about ½ inch x 2 inches.

2. Cut vegetables as follows: cut unpeeled eggplant into matchstick pieces; shred carrot; slice onion; cut bell pepper into matchstick pieces; slice mushrooms; leave bean sprouts whole; shred Chinese cabbage; and cut green onions into 2-inch slivers.

3. Arrange meat and vegetables attractively on a large platter. Have wok oil, teriyaki sauce, and chili sesame oil near cooking area.

4. Allow each guest to select vegetables and lamb from platter. (For each serving, plan on 2 cups of assorted vegetables and ⅓ to ½ cup of meat strips.)

5. Place an electric griddle or skillet over high heat. For each serving add about 2 teaspoons wok oil. Add one serving of meat and vegetables; stir-fry for 3 minutes. Add 3 tablespoons teriyaki sauce; cook, stirring, for 1 minute or until heated through. Season with a few drops of chili sesame oil. Serve hot. Repeat procedure for each serving.

Toishan Veal

(Sweet & Sour Veal in Peppers)

Makes: 4 servings
Preparation time: 10 minutes

Cooking time: 40 minutes

2 large red or green bell peppers

FILLING

¾ pound ground veal

2 green onions (including tops), thinly sliced

3 tablespoons Ginger Flavored Soy Sauce *

⅛ teaspoon Chinese five-spice

1 teaspoon minced garlic

1 teaspoon minced fresh ginger

1 egg, lightly beaten

2 tablespoons dry bread crumbs

¼ pound firm tofu, drained and diced

⅛ teaspoon white pepper

_____

¼ cup Sweet & Sour Stir Fry Sauce *

1. Cut bell peppers in half lengthwise; remove seeds and cores. Blanch pepper shells in boiling water for 1½ minutes; drain. Refresh under cold water and pat dry.

2. Combine filling ingredients in a bowl. Stuff each pepper shell with one-fourth of the filling. Place stuffed peppers, filled side up, in a baking pan.

3. Bake, uncovered, in a 350°F. oven for 35 minutes or until filling is no longer pink when pierced.

4. Brush each pepper with about 1 tablespoon of the stir fry sauce; bake for 5 minutes more.

Comments: Just about any small firm vegetable can become the edible container for this oven-baked veal dish. In the fall, small acorn squashes or miniature pumpkins make wonderful choices. Cut squash in half and remove seeds, or simply cut off the tops of miniature pumpkins (jack-o-lantern style) and scoop out the seeds. Parboil both in boiling water for about 15 minutes to guarantee tenderness, since baking in the oven for 35 minutes isn't quite long enough to cook hard-shell squash.

* **House of Tsang Product**

Tropical Ices

(Assorted Fruit Sorbets)

Makes: 1 quart (each)
Preparation time: 50 minutes (each)

Cooking time: 3 to 5 minutes each
Pictured on: Page 123

TANGERINE-GINGER ICE

1 cup sugar

4 cups fresh tangerine juice (or reconstituted frozen tangerine or orange juice)

4 thin slices fresh ginger

1. Combine sugar, 1 cup of the juice, and ginger in a small stainless steel or enamel saucepan. Boil for 5 minutes. Remove from heat and discard ginger. Let syrup cool.

2. Combine cooled syrup and remaining 3 cups juice in a large bowl. Chill in refrigerator for 20 minutes. Pour into ice cream maker. Freeze according to manufacturer's directions.

HONEYDEW ICE

1 large honeydew melon

1 cup sugar

2 thin slices fresh ginger

2 tablespoons Midori (melon-flavored) liqueur

¼ cup chopped candied ginger

1. Remove seeds and rind from melon; cut melon into 2-inch cubes. Puree melon in a food processor or blender.

2. Combine 1 cup melon puree, sugar, and ginger slices in a small saucepan. Boil for 3 minutes. Remove from heat and discard ginger. Let syrup cool.

3. Combine cooled syrup, the remaining melon puree, and liqueur in a large bowl. Chill in refrigerator for 20 minutes. Pour into ice cream maker. Freeze according to manuafacturer's directions.

4. Top each serving with candied ginger.

STRAWBERRY ICE

½ cup sugar

½ cup water

4 cups fresh strawberries

2 tablespoons Cointreau or other orange-flavored liqueur

1. Combine sugar and water in a small saucepan. Boil for 3 minutes. Remove from heat and let cool.

2. Hull berries; puree in a food processor, blender, or food mill.

3. Combine cooled syrup, strawberry puree, and liqueur in a large bowl. Chill in refrigerator for 20 minutes. Pour into ice cream maker. Freeze according to manufacturer's directions.

*Why choose just one when you can taste a trio of Tropical Ices.
Our assorted fruit sorbet flavors include tangerine-ginger, golden
honeydew and fresh strawberry served with homemade fortune
cookies and Asian Sesame Crisps.*

Make A Fortune

(Homemade Fortune Cookies)

Makes: 1 dozen cookies
Preparation time: 5 minutes

Cooking time: 40 minutes
Pictured on: Page 123

½   cup all-purpose flour

1   tablespoon cornstarch

3   tablespoons sugar

⅛   teaspoon salt

2   large egg whites (about ¼ cup)

¼   cup vegetable oil

½   teaspoon vanilla extract

⅛   teaspoon almond extract

1½ teaspoons water

1. Write special fortune messages on 12 small paper strips that measure approximately 2 inches long and ½-inch wide.

2. Lightly grease a baking sheet and set aside.

3. Combine flour, cornstarch, sugar, and salt in a medium bowl. Add egg whites, vegetable oil, vanilla and almond extracts, and water. Stir into a smooth batter.

4. Bake 3 cookies at a time. For each cookie, spoon 2 teaspoons of batter on prepared baking sheet; spread to make a 3½ to 4-inch circle. Allow 2 inches space between each circle. Bake in a 300°F. oven for 10 to 12 minutes or until light golden brown. Do not overbake.

5. While each cookie is still hot and pliable, remove from pan with a spatula and place on a pot holder. Arrange fortune in center of cookie. Using pot holders to protect your hands, fold cookie in half, then grasp ends of folded cookie and gently pull together. Place folded cookie in muffin pan so that it will keep its shape as it cools.

Comments: If cookies become too cold, they will break when you fold them. If necessary, return baking sheet to oven for 1 minute or until cookies are soft and pliable. Use indelible ink to write messages, so your messages won't run.

Asian Sesame Crisps
(Sesame Cookies)

Makes: 4 dozen cookies
Preparation time: 30 minutes

Cooking time: 10 minutes
Pictured on: Page 123

2¼ cups all-purpose flour

1½ teaspoons baking
powder

1 cup lard or vegetable
shortening

½ cup granulated sugar

½ cup packed brown sugar

1 egg

1 teaspoon vanilla extract

Sesame seeds for coating

1. Sift flour with baking powder into a bowl; set aside.

2. In another bowl, beat lard with granulated sugar and brown sugar until fluffy. Add egg and vanilla extract; beat until well blended. Add flour mixture and blend well.

3. To shape each cookie, roll 1 heaping teaspoon dough into a 1-inch ball. Roll ball in sesame seeds, then place on ungreased baking sheet. Repeat, placing balls about 2 inches apart.

4. Bake in a 350°F. oven for 10 minutes or until lightly browned. Transfer cookies to a wire rack and let cool.

Comments: These crispy, not-too-sweet cookies will stay fresh for several days if you pack them in an air-tight container.

Classical Creations

Recipes for More than 1 hour

Tonight, time is no object. You've planned an impressive menu. The table has been set with candles and flowers, and now you're ready. Delightful, Classical Creations await you.

The key to any successful dinner is timing. But on special occasions, when two or three dishes are being cooked and often served simultaneously, timing is critical so read through each recipe completely.

Experience has taught me to finish the most difficult task first. When planning a menu, I envision each step of a recipe and see how it fits into the overall scheme or order of preparation. For example, Imperial Peking Duck (page 141) served with mandarin pancakes requires more advance preparation than Lobster David (page 149). You'll soon discover how easy it is to prepare won tons (needed for Won Ton Soup, page 133) a day or two in advance.

Time is on your side now. You're well prepared and everything you need—each ingredient or special utensil—is close at hand.

One last bit of advice: Remember that confidence in the kitchen is gained not only through experience, but from the pure pleasure cooking brings to us all. Enjoy.

Foil-wrapped Chicken
(Baked Chicken & Sausage Morsels)

Makes: 16 appetizers
Preparation time: 1 hour

Cooking time: 15 minutes

8 dried black mushrooms
1¼ pounds chicken thighs

MARINADE

2 tablespoons dry sherry
1 tablespoon Ginger
   Flavored Soy Sauce *
2 teaspoons Pure Sesame
   Seed Oil *
2 tablespoons Hoisin
   Sauce *
1 teaspoon minced garlic
1 teaspoon minced fresh
   ginger
⅛ teaspoon Chinese five-
   spice, optional
2 teaspoons cornstarch

16 six-inch squares of foil

2 teaspoons Pure Sesame
   Seed Oil *
1 tablespoon Wok Oil *
1 Chinese sausage (lop
   cheong), cut diagonally
   into 16 slices
⅓ cup sliced bamboo
   shoots
¼ cup chopped red onion

* **House of Tsang Product**

1. Soak mushrooms in enough warm water to cover for 30 minutes; drain. Cut off and discard stems. Cut mushroom caps in half.

2. Remove skin and bone from chicken. Cut meat into bite-size pieces.

3. Combine marinade ingredients in a bowl. Add chicken and mushrooms; stir to coat. Set aside for 30 minutes.

4. Lay squares of foil on work surface. Combine sesame oil and wok oil in a small bowl. Brush oil mixture over each square of foil.

5. To make each packet, place 1 piece of chicken, 1 slice Chinese sausage, and half a mushroom cap in the center of an oiled square of foil. Top with a few bamboo shoot slices and 1 heaping teaspoon chopped onion. Fold foil in half to form a triangle. Double fold cut edges of foil to seal packet. Repeat procedure with remaining ingredients to make 15 more packets.

6. Place packets in a single layer in a shallow rimmed baking pan.

7. Bake in a 375°F. oven for 15 minutes or until juices run clear when chicken is pierced with a fork. (Unfold packet to test for doneness.)

Comments: Tucked inside these small foil-wrapped packages are succulent bits of chicken, sausage, and mushrooms. You can prepare them ahead of time and refrigerate up to 6 hours before baking.

Char Siu Bow

(Steamed Pork Buns)

Makes: 14 buns
Preparation time: 3 hours

Cooking time: 30 minutes

DOUGH

1   package active dry yeast

1   cup warm water (110°F.)

¼   cup sugar

1   teaspoon Pure Sesame Seed Oil *

¾   teaspoon salt

3¼   cups all-purpose flour

FILLING

8   dried black mushrooms

2   tablespoons Wok Oil *

½   teaspoon minced fresh ginger

½   onion, finely chopped

½   cup coarsely chopped water chestnuts

½   cup chicken broth

1   tablespoon Dark Soy Sauce *

¼   cup oyster sauce

2   teaspoons dry sherry

1   tablespoon cornstarch mixed with 1 tablespoon water

1½   cups diced Chinese barbecued pork (recipe page 136 or purchased)

2   green onions (including tops), minced

1. Dissolve yeast in warm water in a large bowl. Add sugar, sesame oil, and salt; let stand in a warm place for 10 minutes or until frothy.

2. Add flour; mix until dough holds together.

3. On a lightly floured surface, knead dough for 5 minutes or until smooth and elastic. Shape into a ball and place in a lightly greased bowl. Cover with a dry towel and let rise in a warm place for 1¼ hours or until doubled in size.

4. Meanwhile, soak mushrooms in enough warm water to cover for 30 minutes; drain. Cut off and discard stems; coarsely chop caps. Set aside.

5. Place a wok or large skillet over medium-high heat until hot. Add wok oil, swirling to coat sides of pan. Add ginger and onion; cook for 2 minutes or until onion is soft. Add mushrooms and water chestnuts; cook for 1 minute.

6. Stir in chicken broth, soy sauce, oyster sauce, and sherry; mix well. Add cornstarch solution and cook, stirring, until sauce boils and thickens slightly. Add barbecued pork and green onions. Remove from heat and let cool.

7. Punch down dough. Roll on a lightly floured surface into a 14-inch long cylinder. Cut crosswise into 1-inch pieces. Shape each piece into a ball; cover and let rest for 5 minutes.

8. To make each bun, roll a ball of dough into a 4-inch circle. Place about 2 tablespoons filling in center of circle. Pull edges of dough over filling; close top by pleating, pinching, and twisting edges together. Place bun, sealed side down, on a 2-inch square of foil. Repeat, to make 13 more buns.

9. Cover buns and let rise in a warm place for 30 minutes or until light and puffed.

10. Arrange one-half of the buns in a single layer, without crowding, in a bamboo steamer. Cover and steam over boiling water for 15 minutes or until tops of buns are glazed and smooth. Repeat to steam remaining buns. Serve warm.

Indonesian Turnovers
(Curried Chicken Dumplings)

Makes: 25 to 30 turnovers
Preparation time: 1 hour

Cooking time: 20 minutes

DOUGH

2 ⅔ cups all-purpose flour

1 teaspoon curry powder

¼ teaspoon salt

1 cup butter or margarine, chilled and diced

About 8 tablespoons ice water

6 dried black mushrooms

¾ pound boneless chicken breasts

MARINADE

1 tablespoon Szechuan Spicy Stir Fry Sauce *

1 teaspoon cornstarch

1. Combine flour, curry powder, and salt in a medium bowl. With a pastry blender or two table knives, cut butter into flour until particles are the size of small peas. Gradually add water until all flour is moistened. With your hands, gather mixture together to form a ball. Cover with plastic wrap and refrigerate for 1 hour.

2. Meanwhile, soak mushrooms in enough warm water to cover for 30 minutes; drain. Cut off and discard stems; finely chop caps. Set aside.

3. Remove skin from chicken and coarsely chop meat. Combine chicken and marinade ingredients in a bowl; stir to coat. Set aside for 15 minutes.

4. Place a wok or large skillet over medium-high heat until hot. Add wok oil, swirling to coat sides of pan. Add chicken, water chestnuts, curry powder, coconut milk, and green onions; stir-fry for 3 minutes. Add cornstarch solution and cook, stirring, until sauce boils and thickens slightly. Remove from heat; let cool. *(Continued)*

2	teaspoons Wok Oil *
¼	cup finely chopped water chestnuts
2	teaspoons curry powder
½	cup coconut milk
2	green onions (including tops), minced
1	teaspoon cornstarch mixed with 2 teaspoons water
1	egg mixed with 1 tablespoon water

*   **House of Tsang Product**

5. Cut pastry dough in half; keep half of the dough covered. Roll out other half on a lightly floured board to ⅛-inch thick. Cut into circles using a 3-inch cutter.

6. To make each turnover, place 2 teaspoons filling in center of circle. Fold dough in half to enclose filling. With a fork, press edges together to seal. Place turnover on an ungreased baking sheet. Repeat procedure with remaining ingredients. Brush tops of turnovers with egg mixture.

7. Bake in a 450°F. oven for 15 minutes or until lightly browned. Serve hot.

Comments: To make dough in a food processor, place flour, curry powder, salt, and chilled butter in a processor bowl. Process for 10 seconds or until lumps are the size of small peas. Add water and process a few seconds longer. (Do not process until mixture forms a ball.) By hand, gather mixture together to form a ball and follow recipe instructions.

Siu Mai
(Steamed Pork Dumplings)

Makes: 30 dumplings
Preparation time: 45 minutes

Cooking time: 36 minutes

FILLING

½   pound lean ground pork

2   tablespoons coarsely chopped water chestnuts

1   green onion (including top), minced

2   tablespoons Ginger Flavored Soy Sauce *

2   teaspoons dry sherry

1   teaspoon Hot Chili Sesame Oil *

1   teaspoon sugar

1   tablespoon cornstarch

½   teaspoon minced garlic

⅛   teaspoon white pepper

1   egg white, lightly beaten

---

30   siu mai or won ton wrappers

Ginger Flavored Soy Sauce *

*   **House of Tsang Product**

1. Combine filling mixture in a bowl; mix well.

2. If using won ton wrappers, trim edges to form a circle and resemble siu mai wrappers. To fill each dumpling, place 2 teaspoons of filling in center of wrapper. Keep wrappers covered as you work to prevent drying. Use fingers to gather up and pleat the wrapper around the filling so dumpling forms an open-topped pouch. Carefully squeeze the middle to give it a waist. Cover filled dumplings with a damp cloth. Repeat procedure with remaining wrappers and filling.

3. Arrange 10 of the dumplings, open side up, without crowding, on a lightly greased 9-inch pie pan. Place pan in a steamer or on a rack in a wok. Cover and steam over boiling water for 10 to 12 minutes or until meat is no longer pink. Keep warm. Repeat with remaining siu mai. Serve dumplings hot with soy sauce for dipping.

Comments: Siu mai is one of the most popular items on a dim sum menu. These dumplings can be cooked ahead and frozen. To reheat, steam frozen dumplings for 10 minutes or until hot.

Sizzling Rice Soup

(Shrimp & Chicken Soup with Rice Crusts)

Makes: 6 servings
Preparation time: 45 minutes

Cooking Time: 1¼ hours

1 cup medium or short-grain rice

1 cup water

6 dried black mushrooms

¼ pound boneless chicken breast

¼ pound medium-size raw shrimp, shelled, deveined, and split in half lengthwise

½ teaspoon salt

½ teaspoon cornstarch

1 teaspoon Pure Sesame Seed Oil *

8 cups chicken broth

2 ounces snow peas, ends and strings removed, cut into slivers

½ cup sliced water chestnuts

2 green onions (including tops), thinly sliced

¼ teaspoon white pepper

Vegetable oil for deep-frying

1 tablespoon Ginger Flavored Soy Sauce *

* **House of Tsang Product**

1. Combine rice and water in a 2-quart saucepan. Cover and bring to a boil over high heat. Reduce heat to low and simmer for 25 minutes. Turn off heat and let stand for 5 minutes. Spread cooked rice in a ¼-inch thick layer in a greased, shallow baking pan. Cut into 1½ to 2-inch squares with a wet knife. Bake in a 350°F. oven for 50 minutes or until rice squares are firm and dry. Set aside 6 squares for soup and store remaining crusts in an air-tight container at room temperature for another use. (Crusts may be stored for up to 6 months.)

2. While cooking rice, soak mushrooms in enough warm water to cover for 30 minutes; drain. Cut off and discard stems; thinly slice caps. Set aside.

3. Remove skin and cut chicken into thin slices.

4. Combine chicken, shrimp, salt, cornstarch, and sesame oil in a bowl; stir to coat. Set aside for 15 minutes.

5. Bring chicken broth to a boil in a large pot. Add mushrooms and chicken and shrimp mixture; cook for 3 minutes or until shrimp turn pink and chicken turns opaque.

6. Add snow peas, water chestnuts, green onions, and white pepper; cook for 1 minute or until snow peas are crisp-tender. Keep warm.

7. Set a wok in a ring stand and add vegetable oil to a depth of about 2 inches. Place over high heat until oil reaches 375°F. on a deep-frying thermometer. Add rice crusts and cook, turning constantly, for 30 seconds or until puffed. Lift out and drain on paper towels.

8. Arrange hot rice crusts in a serving bowl. Immediately pour hot soup over rice crusts so crusts will sizzle. Season with soy sauce.

Won Ton Soup
(Pork Dumplings in Broth)

Makes: 6 servings
Preparation time: 1 hour

Cooking time: 10 minutes

3   dried black mushrooms

FILLING

½   pound ground pork

½   teaspoon minced fresh ginger

1   green onion (including top), minced

1   teaspoon finely chopped cilantro (Chinese parsley)

1   tablespoon Mandarin Marinade *

---

30   won ton wrappers

1   egg, lightly beaten
    Boiling water

8   cups chicken broth

½   cup sliced water chestnuts

½   cup frozen peas, thawed

⅛   teaspoon white pepper

1   teaspoon Hot Chili Sesame Oil *

2   green onions (including tops), thinly sliced

1. Soak mushrooms in enough warm water to cover for 30 minutes; drain. Cut off and discard stems; mince the caps. Combine mushrooms with remaining filling ingredients in a bowl; mix well.

2. To prepare each won ton, place 1 heaping teaspoon of filling in center of each wrapper. Keep wrappers covered as you work to prevent drying. Brush edges of wrapper lightly with egg. Fold in half over filling to form a triangle; press edges firmly to seal. Place filled won ton on a plate and cover with a damp cloth. Repeat procedure with remaining filling and wrappers.

3. Bring a large pot of water to a boil. Add won tons, 10 at a time, and cook for 2 minutes. Remove with a slotted spoon and set aside in a bowl. Repeat procedure until all won tons have been cooked. Discard water.

4. In the same pot, bring chicken broth to a boil. Add water chestnuts, peas, white pepper, and chili sesame oil; cook for 1 minute. Add cooked won tons. Reduce heat and simmer for 1 minute or until won tons are heated through.

5. To serve, ladle into individual soup bowls. Sprinkle with green onions to garnish.

Soto Ayam

(Indonesian Chicken Soup)

Makes: 6 servings
Preparation time: 25 minutes

Cooking time: 1¼ hours

1   tablespoon Wok Oil *
1   medium onion, coarsely chopped
2   teaspoons minced garlic
1   tablespoon minced fresh ginger
2   teaspoons ground coriander
1   teaspoon ground turmeric
½   teaspoon ground cumin
2   pounds chicken legs with thighs attached
6   cups water
2   cups chicken broth
½   teaspoon sugar
¾   teaspoon salt
½   teaspoon white pepper
      Peel from 1 lemon, cut into thin strips
1   tablespoon lemon juice

CONDIMENTS

1½ cups hot, cooked rice or cooked noodles
3   thin-skinned potatoes, boiled, peeled, and thinly sliced
½   cup chopped celery (including leafy ends)
3   hard-cooked eggs, cut into quarters

1. Place a 5-quart pot over medium heat until hot. Add wok oil, swirling to coat bottom of pan. Add onion, garlic, and ginger; cook for 5 minutes or until onion is soft. Add coriander, turmeric, and cumin; cook for 30 seconds. Add chicken, water, chicken broth, sugar, salt, white pepper, and lemon peel. Bring to a boil. Reduce heat, cover, and simmer for 1 hour or until meat near thigh bone is no longer pink when pierced with a knife.

2. Lift out chicken with a slotted spoon and transfer to a plate. Cool slightly. Discard skin and bones; cut chicken into bite-size pieces.

3. Strain broth, discarding seasonings. Skim and discard fat from broth. Return chicken to broth, add lemon juice, and bring to boil.

4. Place condiments in separate bowls to pass at the table. Let each guest half-fill a large soup bowl with condiments. Ladle chicken and broth over condiments. Add fire oil to taste.

1	cup bean sprouts
4	green onions (including tops), thinly sliced
1	lemon, cut into wedges
2	tablespoons Mongolian Fire Oil *

Comments: Indonesian chicken soup is another make-ahead dish that helps busy cooks when friends accept a last-minute invitation to dinner. Prepare the chicken, broth, and bowls of condiments in advance. Then when guests arrive, reheat the broth and set out on the table in a large tureen. Guests assemble their own soup by adding rice or noodles, thin slices of vegetables, and our own Mongolian Fire Oil to taste.

Korean Fire & Ice
(Spicy Korean Chicken Salad)

Makes: 4 to 6 servings
Preparation time: 50 minutes

Cooking time: 16 minutes

1	whole chicken breast
3	tablespoons Korean Teriyaki Sauce *

SALAD

4	cups shredded lettuce
1	small carrot, grated
½	cucumber, peeled, seeded, and cut into matchstick pieces
2	green onions, cut into 1-inch slivers

DRESSING

⅓	cup Korean Teriyaki Sauce *
1½	teaspoons Hot Chili Sesame Oil *
2	tablespoons oil
1	tablespoon vinegar

Cilantro sprigs (Chinese parsley), for garnish

1. Split chicken breast in half. Combine chicken and teriyaki sauce in a bowl. Set aside for 30 minutes.

2. Preheat broiler and adjust rack so chicken will be 3 to 4 inches from heat.

3. Place chicken on a rack in a foil-lined broiling pan, reserving teriyaki sauce. Place under heat and broil, turning once, for 8 minutes on each side or until chicken is cooked through. Baste with reserved teriyaki sauce during last few minutes of broiling.

4. Let chicken cool. Discard bones and skins, then shred meat by hand or with a knife.

5. Combine salad ingredients and chicken in a large bowl.

6. Combine dressing ingredients and toss with salad mixture until well coated. Garnish with cilantro sprigs.

Char Siu
(Chinese Barbecued Pork)

Makes: 1½ pounds
Preparation time: 8½ hours

Cooking time: 40 minutes

2 pounds boneless pork butt or shoulder

MARINADE

3 tablespoons Ginger Flavored Soy Sauce *

3 tablespoons Hoisin Sauce *

1 teaspoon Pure Sesame Seed Oil *

1 tablespoon dry sherry

2 teaspoons sugar

½ teaspoon Chinese five-spice

1 teaspoon minced garlic

GLAZE

2 tablespoons honey

1 tablespoon Hoisin Sauce *

2 teaspoons Hot Chili Sesame Oil *

* **House of Tsang Product**

1. Cut pork, along the grain, into 6-inch lengths. Cut each slice into pieces that measure approximately 3 inches wide and 1½ inches thick. Place meat in a plastic bag or glass container.

2. Combine marinade ingredients in a small bowl. Pour over pork and close bag (or cover container). Refrigerate for 6 hours or overnight. Turn bag over occasionally to distribute flavors.

3. Lift meat from marinade, reserving 2 tablespoons marinade. Place meat on a rack in a foil-lined roasting pan. Roast in a 375°F. oven for 25 minutes.

4. Combine glaze ingredients with reserved marinade in a small bowl. Brush meat on all sides with glaze. Increase heat to 450°F. and continue to roast, brushing occasionally with glaze, for 10 to 15 minutes or until meat is no longer pink when cut in the thickest part. Cut into thin slices and serve hot or at room temperature.

Comments: Cubed or slivered, this versatile meat is delicious as an appetizer and adds a tasty accent to stir-fried rice dishes, soups, and stuffings.

Cantonese Ribs
(Glazed Pork Spareribs)

Makes: 3 or 4 servings
Preparation time: 45 minutes

Cooking time: 65 minutes

2   pounds pork spareribs

MARINADE

¼   cup Ginger Flavored Soy Sauce *

2   tablespoons dry sherry

3   tablespoons ketchup

2   teaspoons minced garlic

2   teaspoons sugar

¼   teaspoon Chinese five-spice

GLAZE

3   tablespoons Hoisin Sauce *

1   tablespoon Pure Sesame Seed Oil *

*   **House of Tsang Product**

1. Trim and discard excess fat from spareribs. Lightly score surface of ribs with a sharp knife.

2. Combine marinade ingredients in a large bowl. Add spareribs, turning to coat all sides. Set aside for 30 minutes, or cover and refrigerate overnight.

3. Combine glaze ingredients in a small bowl and set aside.

4. Drain ribs, reserving marinade. Place ribs on a rack in a foil-lined baking pan. Bake in a 350°F. oven for 30 minutes. Turn meat over, baste with reserved marinade, and continue to bake for 30 minutes or until tender when pierced with a knife.

5. Adjust oven rack so spareribs will be 3 to 4 inches from heat.

6. Brush glaze on both sides of ribs. Place under heat and broil for 2 to 3 minutes on each side or until richly glazed.

Comments: Pork spareribs first marinate in a mixture of ketchup, sherry, soy sauce, and Chinese five-spice before they are quickly broiled (or barbecued) and basted with a delicious glaze made with hoisin sauce and sesame oil. Double the recipe — leftovers make an easy addition to last-minute picnics or backyard meals.

Red-cooked Lamb

(Braised Lamb Stew)

Makes: 4 to 6 servings
Preparation time: 15 minutes

Cooking time: 50 minutes

1½ pounds boneless lamb stew meat (shoulder or neck), cut into 1-inch cubes

½ teaspoon salt

⅛ teaspoon white pepper

¼ cup all-purpose flour

1 tablespoon Wok Oil *

2 cups chicken broth

1 teaspoon minced garlic

1 teaspoon minced fresh ginger

2 whole star anise

3 tablespoons Dark Soy Sauce *

2 onions, each cut into 8 wedges

3 russet potatoes, peeled and cut into 2-inch cubes

2 green onions (including tops), cut into 2-inch lengths

1½ teaspoons Mongolian Fire Oil *

1. Season lamb with salt and pepper. Dredge meat in flour; shake off excess flour.

2. Place a 3-quart saucepan over high heat until hot. Add wok oil, swirling to coat bottom of pan. Add lamb; cook until browned on all sides. Add chicken broth, garlic, ginger, star anise, soy sauce, onions, potatoes, and green onions. Bring to a boil. Reduce heat, cover, and simmer for 45 minutes or until meat is tender and vegetables are soft. Discard star anise. Stir in fire oil and serve.

Comments: Serve this one-dish meal with crusty bread and a tossed green salad.

*   **House of Tsang Product**

Repeat Performance
(Oxtail & Daikon Casserole)

Makes: 6 to 8 servings
Preparation time: 35 minutes

Cooking time: 2¼ hours

2	pieces dried tangerine peel
2	whole star anise
6	thin slices fresh ginger
3	pounds oxtail, cut into 2-inch thick slices
1	tablespoon Wok Oil *
½	teaspoon white pepper
2	teaspoons sugar
¼	cup Dark Soy Sauce *
3	cups beef broth or water
1	onion, cut into 1-inch pieces
4	carrots, cut into ½-inch thick slices
2	stalks celery, cut into 1-inch pieces
1	pound daikon, cut into 1 x 2-inch pieces
3	tablespoons cornstarch mixed with ⅓ cup water

Hot cooked rice

* **House of Tsang Product**

1. Soak tangerine peel in enough warm water to cover for 5 minutes; drain and set aside.

2. Tie star anise, ginger, and tangerine peel in a piece of cheesecloth; set aside.

3. Remove excess fat from oxtail. Place oxtail in a large pot in warm water to cover and bring to a boil. Reduce heat and simmer for 5 minutes; drain well.

4. Place a large pot over medium-high heat until hot. Add wok oil, swirling to coat bottom of pan. Add white pepper and blanched oxtail. Cook for 8 to 10 minutes or until oxtail pieces are browned on all sides. Add sugar and soy sauce; cook for 2 minutes. Add beef broth and reserved cheesecloth bundle; bring to a boil. Reduce heat, cover, and simmer for 1¾ hours.

5. Add onion, carrots, celery, and daikon. Simmer for 30 minutes or until oxtail and vegetables are tender.

6. Add cornstarch solution and cook, stirring, until sauce boils and thickens slightly. Serve over hot cooked rice.

Comments: As with most casseroles, leftovers taste even better.

Mandarin Pancakes
(Thin Chinese Pancakes)

Makes: About 16 pancakes
Preparation time: 1 hour

Cooking time: 30 minutes

2   cups all-purpose flour
¼   teaspoon salt
¾   cup boiling water
2   tablespoons Hot Chili
     Sesame Oil *

*   **House of Tsang Product**

1. Place flour and salt in a medium bowl. Add boiling water; stir until dough holds together. On a lightly floured surface, knead dough for 5 minutes or until smooth and satiny. Cover with a damp cloth and let rest for 30 minutes.

2. On a lightly floured surface, roll dough into a 16-inch long cylinder. Cut cylinder crosswise into 1-inch pieces. Shape each piece into a ball, then flatten slightly into a 3-inch pancake. To make a pair of pancakes, brush the top of two 3-inch pancakes with a light coating of chili sesame oil. Place one pancake on top of a second pancake, oiled sides together. Using a rolling pin, roll the 2 pancakes together to make a circle 6 inches in diameter. Cover with a damp cloth and set aside. Repeat procedure to make remaining pancakes.

3. Place an ungreased skillet with a nonstick finish over low heat. Add one double pancake and cook for 2 minutes. Turn over and cook for 2 minutes more or until bubbles appear on the surface and pancakes are lightly browned. Remove from pan and separate into 2 pancakes while still hot. Stack cooked pancakes on a plate and repeat procedure with remaining double pancakes. Serve with dishes such as Mu Shu Pork (page 119), Imperial Peking Duck (page 141), and Critic's Choice (page 146).

Imperial Peking Duck

(Peking Duck)

Makes: 4 to 6 servings
Preparation time: 9 hours

Cooking time: 1 hour

2	teaspoons salt
¼	teaspoon Chinese five-spice
1	teaspoon minced fresh ginger
2	teaspoons minced garlic
1	duckling (4 to 5 lbs.), head intact
1	whole star anise
2	sprigs cilantro (Chinese parsley)

GLAZE

8	cups water
3	tablespoons honey
½	cup cider vinegar
½	cup cornstarch mixed with 1 cup water

¼	cup Hoisin Sauce *
4	green onions (including tops), cut into 2-inch pieces
12	Mandarin pancakes (recipe page 140 or purchased)

* **House of Tsang Product**

1. Combine salt, five-spice, ginger, and garlic in a bowl. Rub cavity of duck with mixture. Place star anise and cilantro inside cavity. Sew the tail cavity shut with heavy thread or securely fasten opening with a skewer. Loop a piece of string around duck neck allowing enough string to make a hanging loop. (If duck does not have a head, sew opening with string and allow enough extra string to make a hanging loop.)

2. Bring 4 quarts of water to a boil in a large pot. Slowly lower duck into boiling water. Let boil for 2 minutes. Remove duck and hang to dry.

3. To make glaze, bring water and honey to a boil in a 3-quart pan. Add vinegar. Slowly stir in cornstarch solution and cook, stirring constantly, until glaze boils and thickens.

4. Holding duck by the head or neck string, brush glazing marinade evenly over the bird. Repeat 3 or 4 times or until well-coated.

5. Hang glazed duck in a cool, airy dry place for 8 hours or until skin is dry (or place duck on a rack in a roasting pan and refrigerate, uncovered, for 2 days).

6. Place duck on a rack in a foil-lined roasting pan. Roast in a 425°F. oven for 20 minutes. Reduce heat to 350°F. Continue to roast for 40 to 45 minutes or until skin is richly browned and juices run clear when a knife is inserted into thigh.

7. Remove duck from oven; let stand for 5 minutes. Transfer duck to another pan. Cut the string and let the juices from the cavity drain into the pan.

(Continued)

Remove cilantro and star anise. Transfer duck to a cutting board. With a sharp paring knife, slice skin with a small amount of meat underneath and place on a platter.

8. To assemble each serving, spread a small amount of hoisin sauce on a pancake, top with a piece of duck and a few slices of green onion, then wrap pancake around filling. Serve warm.

Nesting Chicken
(Chicken in a Potato Basket)

Makes: 4 to 6 servings
Preparation time: 50 minutes

Cooking time: 15 minutes

¾ pound boneless chicken breasts

MARINADE

2 tablespoons Ginger Flavored Soy Sauce *

1 tablespoon dry sherry

2 teaspoons cornstarch

_____

½ teaspoon salt

2 russet potatoes (about ¾ lb. total)

Vegetable oil for deep-frying

¼ pound snow peas, ends and strings removed

1 can (6¾ oz.) straw mushrooms, drained

1 can (8¾ oz.) baby corn, drained and cut in half

1 can (about 1½ oz.) quail eggs, drained

¼ cup sliced water chestnuts

1. Remove skin from chicken and cut meat into bite-size pieces. Combine chicken and marinade ingredients in a small bowl; stir to coat. Set aside for 15 minutes.

2. Fill a large bowl with water; stir in salt. Peel potatoes, then cut into 2-inch matchstick pieces. Place in salted water and set aside until ready to cook.

3. Drain potatoes thoroughly and pat dry with paper towels. Set wok in a ring stand and add vegetable oil to a depth of about 2 inches. Place over medium-high heat until oil reaches 360°F. on a deep-frying thermometer. Spread half the potatoes evenly over sides and bottom of a lightly oiled wire strainer. Press a second wire strainer of the same size down into the first to form a potato "nest".

4. Holding strainers together, lower basket into the oil and fry, carefully ladling oil over all sides, until evenly browned. Remove from oil and gently tap strainers to loosen "nest". Remove potato "nest" from strainer and drain on paper

SAUCE

⅔ cup chicken broth

1 tablespoon Dark Soy Sauce *

2 tablespoons oyster sauce

——————

2½ teaspoons cornstarch mixed with 2 tablespoons water

¾ cup chopped walnuts

Lettuce leaves, for garnish

towels. Repeat with remaining potatoes. Set nests aside.

5. Remove all but 1½ tablespoons oil from wok. Reheat oil over high heat until hot. Add chicken; stir-fry for 2 minutes. Add snow peas; stir-fry for 1 minute. Add straw mushrooms, baby corn, quail eggs, water chestnuts, and sauce ingredients. Bring to a boil and cook for 3 minutes or until snow peas are crisp-tender. Add cornstarch solution and cook, stirring, until sauce boils and thickens slightly. Remove from heat. Add walnuts and toss to mix.

6. To serve, place potato nests on a lettuce-lined platter. Fill each nest with half the chicken mixture. Serve hot.

————————

Golden Phoenix
(Rice-filled Whole Chicken)

Makes: 6 to 8 servings
Preparation time: Overnight

Cooking time: 2 hours

MARINADE

20 Szechuan peppercorns

2 tablespoons dry sherry

3 tablespoons Ginger Flavored Soy Sauce *

2 whole star anise

1 roasting chicken (4 to 4½ lbs.)

STUFFING

¾ cup glutinous rice

1 cup water

1. In a wide frying pan, toast peppercorns over medium-high heat for 5 minutes or until fragrant, shaking pan frequently. Use a mortar and pestle to grind to a powder and measure ½ teaspoon for marinade.

2. Combine ground peppercorn and remaining marinade ingredients in a large bowl. Add chicken; turn to coat all sides. Cover and refrigerate for 8 hours or overnight.

3. Place rice in a 1-quart pot. Add water. Bring to a boil over medium-high heat. Boil, uncovered, for 10 minutes or until water evaporates and crater-like holes appear. Reduce heat, cover, and steam rice for 20 minutes.

(continued)

4	dried black mushrooms
2	tablespoons dried shrimp
1	tablespoon Wok Oil *
2	Chinese sausages (lop cheong), diced
1	small carrot, diced
¼	cup frozen peas, thawed
2	green onions (including tops), minced
½	teaspoon salt
¼	teaspoon white pepper
1	teaspoon Pure Sesame Seed Oil *

SAUCE

	About ¾ cup chicken broth
2	tablespoons Ginger Flavored Soy Sauce *
1½	tablespoons cornstarch mixed with 3 table- spoons water
1	teaspoon sugar
⅛	teaspoon white pepper

* **House of Tsang Product**

4. Meanwhile, in separate bowls, soak mushrooms and shrimp in enough warm water to cover for 30 minutes; drain. Cut off and discard mushroom stems; dice caps and set aside. Drain shrimp. Coarsely chop and set aside.

5. Place a wok or large skillet over medium-high heat until hot. Add wok oil, swirling to coat sides of pan. Add Chinese sausages, mushrooms, and shrimp; stir-fry for 1 minute. Add carrot, peas, green onions, cooked rice, salt, and white pep-per; stir-fry for 2 minutes or until carrot is crisp-tender. Let cool.

6. Remove chicken from marinade. Fill breast cavity with rice stuffing. Overlap skin and secure with small metal skewers or sew cavity closed.

7. Place chicken, breast side up, on a rack in a foil-lined roasting pan. Tie legs together. Roast in a 350°F. oven for 1½ hours or until juices run clear when meat near thigh bone is pierced with a knife.

8. Transfer chicken to a platter. Remove string and skewers. Remove stuffing from cavity and place in a serving bowl. Brush sesame oil over chicken. Keep warm while preparing sauce.

9. Pour pan drippings into a 2-cup measure. Skim off and discard fat. Add enough chicken broth to make 1¼ cups liquid. Pour into a small saucepan. Add remaining sauce ingredients; mix well. Place saucepan over medium heat, stirring occasion-ally, and bring to a boil. Pour sauce into a serving bowl. Serve with the chicken.

Chinese Chicken in Clay

(Chicken Cooked in a Clay Pot)

Makes: 8 servings
Preparation time: 30 minutes

Cooking time: 45 minutes

10 dried black mushrooms
1 pound boneless chicken thighs or breasts

MARINADE

1 tablespoon Mandarin Marinade *
1 tablespoon dry sherry
1 teaspoon minced fresh ginger
1 teaspoon cornstarch

———————

2 teaspoons Wok Oil *
½ teaspoon minced fresh ginger
2 Chinese sausages (lop cheong), sliced diagonally into ¼-inch thick slices
2 tablespoons oyster sauce
¼ cup sliced Szechuan preserved vegetable (optional)
2 teaspoons Pure Sesame Seed Oil *
2 cups uncooked long-grain rice
2¼ cups water

3 green onions (including tops), thinly sliced
    Cilantro sprigs

1. Soak mushrooms in enough warm water to cover for 30 minutes; drain. Cut off and discard stems; cut caps into quarters. Set aside.

2. Remove skin from chicken and cut meat into 1-inch x 3-inch pieces. Combine marinade ingredients in a large bowl. Add chicken; stir to coat. Set aside for 15 minutes.

3. Place a wok or large skillet over medium-high heat until hot. Add wok oil, swirling to coat sides of pan. Add ginger and cook until fragrant. Add chicken; stir-fry for 2 minutes. Add Chinese sausages and mushrooms; stir-fry for 2 minutes. Add oyster sauce and preserved vegetable; cook for 1 minute or until chicken begins to turn opaque. Stir in sesame oil. Set aside.

4. Place rice in a 2-quart clay pot or saucepan. Add water and bring to a boil over medium-low to medium heat. Increase heat to medium-high and boil, uncovered, for 10 minutes or until water evaporates and crater-like holes appear.

5. Place chicken-sausage mixture over rice. Cover and simmer over low heat for 25 minutes or until rice is tender and all liquid is absorbed.

6. Sprinkle green onions and cilantro sprigs over rice before serving directly from clay pot.

Critic's Choice
(Tea-smoked Chicken)

Makes: 6 servings
Preparation time: Overnight

Cooking time: About 1½ hours
Pictured on: Page 147

MARINADE

3 green onions (including tops), cut in half

4 thin slices fresh ginger

2 whole star anise, broken into pieces

3 tablespoons Dark Soy Sauce *

2 tablespoons dry sherry

1 teaspoon salt

1 teaspoon Szechuan peppercorns (or ½ teaspoon ground white pepper)

¾ teaspoon sugar

¼ teaspoon Chinese five-spice

———————

1 frying chicken (3 to 4 lbs.)

½ cup black tea leaves

⅓ cup packed brown sugar

½ cup uncooked rice

Green onion slivers, for garnish

* **House of Tsang Product**

1. Combine marinade ingredients in a large bowl. Rub chicken inside and out with marinade. Cover and refrigerate overnight.

2. Remove chicken from bowl. Tightly wrap chicken in foil. Place in a baking pan and bake in a 450°F. oven for 40 minutes or until juices run clear when thigh is pierced with a knife. Unwrap chicken and let cool. (Chicken can also be steamed: place chicken, breast side up, on a heat-proof dish. Set dish in a steamer or on a rack in a wok. Cover and steam over boiling water for 1 hour. Remove from steamer and let cool.)

3. Meanwhile, line a large wok and its lid with foil. Combine tea leaves, sugar, and rice, and place on bottom of the foil-lined wok. Set a rack in the wok.

4. Place chicken, breast side up, on top of the rack. Cover with foil-lined lid. Cook over high heat for 2 minutes; turn off heat for 5 minutes. Cook for 2 minutes more; turn off heat for 5 minutes. Repeat cooking procedure 5 or 6 times. Do not remove lid during smoking process. Let stand after final turn, covered, for several minutes to allow smoke to subside.

5. Remove chicken and cut into serving pieces. Arrange chicken on a serving platter and sprinkle with green onion slivers.

Tea-smoked chicken is the Critic's Choice for a most unusual and festive dish. Marinated whole chicken smokes in a covered wok directly over a mixture of black tea leaves, brown sugar and uncooked rice. Serve warm or at room temperature with Mandarin pancakes or steamed Chinese buns.

Show Stoppers

(Chicken, Ham & Baby Bok Choy)

Makes: 4 servings
Preparation time: 15 minutes

Cooking time: 55 minutes

1   frying chicken
(3 to 4 lbs.)

6   thin slices fresh ginger

2   green onions (including tops)

2   teaspoons salt

2   teaspoons Pure Sesame Seed Oil*

2   slices Smithfield or Virginia ham (about ½ lb.), cut ¼-inch thick

1   pound baby bok choy

½   teaspoon white pepper

1   tablespoon cornstarch mixed with 2 tablespoons water

*   **House of Tsang Product**

1. Place chicken in a 4-quart saucepan. Add ginger, green onions, salt, and enough water to barely cover chicken. Bring to a boil. Cover and simmer over medium-low heat for 45 minutes or until meat near thigh bone is no longer pink when pierced.

2. Carefully remove chicken from pot, reserving broth. Let cool briefly. Rub sesame oil over chicken. Cut chicken into serving pieces, removing bones, if desired; set aside.

3. Skim fat from chicken broth. Place 3 cups broth in a saucepan. Add ham; simmer for 5 minutes. Remove ham from broth and cut into 1½-inch squares. Set aside ham and reserve broth.

4. Arrange 8 bok choy leaves attractively on an oval platter. Cut remaining bok choy in half lengthwise. Place in reserved broth; simmer for 1 minute or until crisp-tender. Remove bok choy with a slotted spoon; drain well. Arrange around edge of platter. Reserve 1 cup of broth for sauce.

5. Arrange alternating pieces of chicken and ham over bok choy.

6. Bring 1 cup reserved broth and white pepper to a boil in a small saucepan. Add cornstarch solution and cook, stirring, until sauce boils and thickens slightly. Pour warm sauce over chicken and ham.

Lobster David
(Cantonese-style Lobster)

Makes: 4 to 6 servings
Preparation time: 50 minutes

Cooking time: 11 minutes

MARINADE

1 tablespoon dry sherry

2 teaspoons cornstarch

1 teaspoon Pure Sesame Seed Oil *

1 tablespoon Ginger Flavored Soy Sauce *

———————

¼ pound ground pork

3 lobster tails (about 2 lbs. total)

2 tablespoons Wok Oil *

2 tablespoons dry sherry

2 tablespoons fermented black beans, rinsed, and finely chopped

1 teaspoon minced garlic

2 teaspoons minced ginger

1 cup chicken broth

3 tablespoons Dark Soy Sauce *

1 teaspoon crushed red pepper

½ teaspoon sugar

¼ cup frozen peas, thawed

1½ tablespoons cornstarch mixed with 3 tablespoons water

2 teaspoons Hot Chili Sesame Oil *

3 egg whites, beaten

3 green onions, sliced

1. Combine marinade ingredients in a small bowl. Add pork; stir to coat. Set aside for 30 minutes.

2. Cut lobster tails in half lengthwise and devein. Cut each half into 4 pieces with shells attached.

3. Place a wok or large skillet over high heat until hot. Add wok oil, swirling to coat sides of pan. Add lobster; stir-fry for 1 minute. Add sherry; cook, covered, for 3 to 4 minutes or until lobster shells turn red. Remove lobster with a slotted spoon and set aside.

4. Add black beans, garlic, and ginger to wok; cook, stirring, until fragrant. Add pork; cook, stirring, for 2 minutes. Return lobster to wok. Add chicken broth, soy sauce, crushed red pepper, and sugar. Simmer, covered, for 3 minutes. Add peas; cook for 1 minute.

5. Add cornstarch solution and cook, stirring, until sauce boils and thickens slightly. Remove from heat. Stir in chili sesame oil and egg whites; stir until egg whites form long threads.

6. Transfer to a serving platter, sprinkle with green onions, and serve hot.

Comments: Here's a delightful dish for entertaining special friends. Since the cooking time is short, prepare everything in advance, then stir-fry at the last minute.

Not your ordinary Catch-of-the-Day, braised whole trout encases a wonderful, ginger-flavored stuffing made from shrimp, black mushrooms, and water chestnuts. Garnish with slivers of green onion and bamboo shoots, and sprigs of cilantro.

Catch-of-the-Day

(Braised Trout with Seafood Stuffing)

Makes: 2 to 4 servings
Preparation time: 60 minutes

Cooking time: 13 minutes
Pictured on: Page 150

STUFFING

8	dried black mushrooms
¼	cup sliced water chestnuts
½	pound white fish fillets, cut into bite-size pieces
½	pound medium-size raw shrimp, shelled and deveined
1	teaspoon minced fresh ginger
½	teaspoon minced garlic
1	egg white
2	teaspoons cornstarch
1	tablespoon dry sherry
1	tablespoon Ginger Flavored Soy Sauce *
½	teaspoon Pure Sesame Seed Oil *
¼	teaspoon white pepper
¼	teaspoon salt

2	trout (each about ½ lb.), boned, with head left intact
	Salt
	Cornstarch for dry-coating
2	tablespoons Wok Oil *
¼	cup shredded bamboo shoots
⅔	cup chicken broth

1. Soak mushrooms in enough warm water to cover for 30 minutes; drain. Cut off and discard stems. Finely chop half of the mushrooms and then thinly slice remaining mushrooms; set both aside.

2. In food processor, process water chestnuts until coarsely chopped. Add fish fillets, shrimp, ginger, and garlic and process to make a rough paste. To make without a food processor, finely chop with a heavy knife. Combine fish paste and chopped mushrooms in a bowl. Stir in egg white, cornstarch, sherry, soy sauce, sesame oil, white pepper, and salt; blend well.

3. Lightly sprinkle trout with salt. Fill each trout with half of the stuffing mixture. Dust both sides of fish lightly with cornstarch.

4. Place a wide frying pan with a nonstick finish over medium-high heat. Add wok oil, swirling to coat bottom of pan. Add trout and saute, uncovered, for 3 to 4 minutes on each side or until golden brown.

5. Sprinkle fish with remaining sliced mushrooms and bamboo shoots. Add chicken broth. Cover and simmer for 15 minutes or until stuffing is firm and opaque. With a slotted spatula, lift fish to a warm platter.

6. To the pan, add dark soy sauce and cornstarch solution and cook, stirring, until sauce boils and thickens slightly. Stir in green onions and chili sesame oil. Spoon over fish.

(Continued)

1 tablespoon Dark Soy
Sauce *

1 tablespoon cornstarch
mixed with 2 table-
spoons water

2 green onions (including
tops), cut into 2-inch
lengths and slivered

2 teaspoons Hot Chili
Sesame Oil *

* **House of Tsang Product**

Comments: The Chinese word for fish is pro-
nounced "yu" and is the same word used for "remain" or "abundance". For this reason, it is a
Chinese tradition to serve whole fish during Chinese New Years and other happy occasions. To
honor a guest, the host at the Chinese dinner will
always serve fish with the head pointed in the
direction of the guest of honor. A whole fish
served at a party guarantees that friendship,
happiness, and good fortune felt by the guests
will "remain" for a long time.

Emperor's Secret
(Wok-smoked Salmon Steaks)

Makes: 4 servings
Preparation time: 4 hours

Cooking time: 13 minutes

MARINADE

⅓ cup Ginger Flavored Soy
Sauce *

3 tablespoons dry sherry

1 green onion (including
top), minced

---

4 salmon steaks, each
about ¾-inch thick
(about 1½ lbs. total)

SMOKING MIXTURE

¼ cup black tea leaves

3 tablespoons brown sugar

¼ cup uncooked rice

2 whole star anise

1. Combine marinade ingredients in a shallow glass
dish that will hold salmon in one layer. Add
salmon; turn to coat both sides. Cover and refrigerate for 4 to 6 hours.

2. Line a large wok and its lid with foil. Place smoking mixture in foil-lined wok; mix well. Set a rack
in the wok.

3. Drain and discard marinade, including onion.
Arrange salmon in a single layer in a heatproof
dish that will fit on the rack. Place dish on top of
the rack. Cover with foil-lined lid. Cook over
medium-high heat for 5 minutes; turn off heat
for 3 minutes. Cook for 5 minutes more. Let
stand, covered, for several minutes to allow
smoke to subside.

4. Transfer salmon to a serving platter. Sprinkle
with green onion slivers. Serve at room temperature.

1 teaspoon Szechuan
peppercorns

———————

Green onion slivers, for
garnish

Comments: Although this well-known fish dish from Shanghai looks like it has been smoked, it is actually deep-fried, marinated, and deep-fried again. But in this easy-to-make version, salmon steaks are cooked by seasoned smoke in a wok. Serve hot as an entree or cold as an appetizer.

Heavenly Cloud
(Almond-Coconut Gelatin)

Makes: 6 to 8 servings
Preparation time: 3½ hours

Cooking time: 4 minutes

2 cups water

1⅓ cups milk

2 envelopes (¼ oz. each) unflavored gelatin

1½ tablespoons sugar

2 teaspoons almond extract

1½ teaspoons coconut extract

SYRUP

1 cup water

⅓ cup sugar

½ teaspoon almond extract

FRUIT FOR GARNISH

Lychee

Pineapple cubes

Kiwi fruit slices

Mandarin orange segments

Maraschino cherries

1. Combine water, milk, gelatin, and sugar in a small saucepan; heat to simmering. Cook, stirring, until sugar and gelatin are dissolved. Remove from heat and stir in almond and coconut extracts.

2. Pour mixture into an 8-inch square pan and refrigerate for 3 hours or until firm.

3. To make syrup, combine water and sugar in a small saucepan; bring to a boil. Cook for 3 minutes. Stir in almond extract. Let cool, then refrigerate until ready to serve.

4. To serve, cut almond-coconut gelatin into small squares or diamond shapes; place in individual bowls. Arrange fruit attractively around gelatin. Spoon some of the syrup over fruit and gelatin; offer remaining syrup at the table.

Comments: A simple, make-ahead light dessert combines the flavors of almond and coconut garnished with fresh (or canned) fruit.

Tsang Tarts

(Individual Lemon Custard Tarts)

Makes: 14 to 16 tarts
Preparation time: 2½ hours

Cooking time: 35 minutes
Pictured on: Page 155

PASTRY DOUGH

½	cup lard, chilled and diced
¼	cup unsalted butter, chilled and diced
1	egg
1¾	cups all-purpose flour
1	teaspoon vanilla extract
2	tablespoons ice water

FILLING

⅔	cup sugar
⅔	cup boiling water
⅓	cup evaporated milk
4	eggs, lightly beaten
2½	teaspoons grated lemon peel
½	teaspoon vanilla extract
1	teaspoon lemon extract

1. Place chilled lard, butter, and egg in a food processor. Process for 3 to 4 seconds. Add flour and process until lumps are the size of peas. Add vanilla and water and process a few seconds longer. (Do Not Over Process.) Mixture should be lumpy. Press crumbs together and wrap with plastic wrap. Chill for 45 minutes.

2. On a lightly floured board, roll out dough ¼-inch thick to form a rectangle.
   Fold the rectangle of dough into thirds, as if folding a letter, then turn dough 90 degrees. Roll out again into a rectangle to ¼-inch thick and fold into thirds. Cover with plastic wrap. Let dough rest in refrigerator for 20 minutes.

3. Meanwhile, prepare filling. In a large bowl, dissolve sugar in boiling water; let cool to room temperature. Whisk in evaporated milk and eggs. Stir in lemon peel and vanilla and lemon extracts.

4. Remove chilled dough from refrigerator; place on a lightly floured board. Roll out dough into a large rectangle about ¼-inch thick. With a 4-inch diameter cookie cutter, cut out a dozen or more circles. Center each pastry circle in a 2½-inch tart tin. Lightly press dough into bottom and sides of tin; trim edges. Chill for 1 hour or overnight.

5. Remove pastry-lined tins from refrigerator. Pour filling into pastry-lined tins to within ¼-inch of the top. Place filled tins on a cookie sheet; bake in a 300°F. oven for 35 minutes or until a knife inserted in center comes out clean. Cool slightly. Turn tins upside down, gently tapping to release crust. Cool, custard side up, on a wire rack. Serve warm.

Individual lemon custard tarts are the featured attraction at this afternoon tea party. Serve Tsang Tarts with assorted dried fruit, nuts, candies, and purchased cookies, as pictured, or all by themselves.

Eight Treasures

(Sweet Rice Pudding)

Makes: 6 servings
Preparation time: 40 minutes

Cooking time: 1½ hours

2 cups glutinous rice

2 cups water

1 walnut-size piece rock sugar (or 1½ teaspoons sugar)

1 slice candied pineapple

10 dried figs

10 dried apricot halves

12 pitted dates

12 candied red cherries

⅔ cup sweet bean paste

2 tablespoons raisins

SYRUP

1 can (8¼ oz.) sliced pineapple packed in heavy syrup

½ cup water

3 walnut-size pieces rock sugar (or 1½ table-spoons sugar)

1. Soak rice in enough water to cover for 30 minutes; drain. Transfer rice to a medium saucepan. Add the 2 cups water and 1 piece rock sugar. Bring to a boil over medium-high heat. Boil, uncovered, for 10 minutes or until water evaporates and crater-like holes appear. Reduce heat, cover, and simmer for 25 minutes. Let cool for 15 minutes.

2. Lightly grease a 1-quart heatproof bowl with vegetable oil. Place candied pineapple slice in center of bottom of bowl. Arrange figs and apricots attractively around pineapple. Place dates and cherries alternately around fruit and up the sides of the bowl.

3. Carefully spread half of the cooked rice over the fruit, pressing down lightly. Spread bean paste evenly over rice. Cover with half of the remaining rice. Sprinkle raisins over rice. Top with remaining rice, pressing down firmly. Cover bowl with a small damp cloth.

4. Place bowl in a steamer or on a rack in a wok; cover and steam over boiling water for 1 hour, adding water to steamer if necessary. Remove bowl from steamer; let cool for 10 minutes.

5. While rice is steaming, prepare syrup. Drain pineapple slices, reserving syrup. Cut into bite-size pieces; set aside. Heat water, rock sugar, and reserved pineapple syrup in a small saucepan until sugar dissolves; simmer for 5 minutes. Add pineapple pieces to pan; keep warm.
Cover mold with a serving platter and invert, gently shaking, to unmold. Spoon hot syrup over pudding. Serve hot.

About Chef David Tsang

Without a doubt, David Tsang has one of the most unusual backgrounds of any Oriental chef. Although he worked for years as an engineering physicist at Stanford University, his great passion for Oriental cooking and his entrepreneurial spirit eventually pried him away from science.

In 1975, he founded Tsang & Ma, one of the first companies in the United States to distribute a variety of Oriental vegetable seeds nationwide. He soon expanded his line to include Oriental cookware and later introduced the successful line of HOUSE OF TSANG seasoning oils, sauces, and spices.

For the past 12 years, David Tsang has been instrumental in popularizing Oriental cooking in the United States. His contributions range from innovative food products to new ideas in the Oriental restaurant business. A tireless advocate of Chinese cuisine, David brings his message to cooking schools and television and radio audiences across the country.

Index

A
Almond-Coconut Gelatin, 153
Appetizer, Spicy Asparagus, 42
Appetizers, Sesame-coated Cream Cheese, 41
Asian Beef, 93
Asian Sesame Crisps, 125
Asparagus, Spicy Appetizer, 42
Assorted Fruit Sorbets, 122

B
Baby Corn, 20
Bacon Burgers, Oriental, 92
Baked Chicken & Sausage Morsels, 127
Bamboo Shoots, 20
Bean Thread Noodles, 10, 24
Beef & Asparagus in Black Bean Sauce, 93
Beef & Green Onions, Skewered, 66
Beer, 35, 36
Beijing Burgers, 92

Belles & Beef, 63
Black Bean Sauce, Beef & Asparagus in, 93
Black & White Pyramids, 41
Blue Plate Special, 64
Bombay Madness, 108
Brandied Kiwi & Oranges, 101
Braised Lamb Stew, 138
Braised Orange-flavored Ribs, 117
Braised Straw, Button & Black Mushrooms, 111
Braised Trout with Seafood Stuffing, 151
Broccoli with Oyster Sauce, 44
Broiled Honey-Ginger Chicken Wings, 109
Bronze Swimmer, 58

C
Cabbage, Chinese (Napa), 10, 20
Candied Ginger, 22

Candied Ginger Sauce, Pears with, 100
Cantonese Ribs, 137
Cantonese-style Lobster, 149
Cashew Chicken, 85
Catch-of-the-Day, 151
Char Siu, 136
Char Siu Bow, 128
Chicken Cooked in a Clay Pot, 145
Chicken Dumplings, Curried, 129
Chicken Drummets, Five-spice, 84
Chicken, Ham & Baby Bok Choy, 148
Chicken in a Potato Basket, 142
Chicken Power, 53
Chicken, Rice-filled Whole, 143
Chicken Salad, Spicy Korean, 135
Chicken & Sausage Morsels, Baked, 127

Chicken Soup, Indonesian, 134
Chicken, Sweet & Sour with
  Oranges, 50
Chicken, Tea-smoked, 146
Chicken Teriyaki, Stir-fried
  over Rice, 81
Chicken & Tofu, Curried, 53
Chicken & Vegetables, Spicy, 47
Chicken Wings, Broiled Honey-
  Ginger, 109
Chili-flavored Crab with Silver
  Noodles, 90
Chili-flavored Potato Salad, 73
Chili Oil, 10, 20
China, Culinary Regions of, 7
Chinese Barbecued Pork, 136
Chinese Chicken in Clay, 145
Chinese Eggplant, 10, 22
Chinese Five-Spice, 22
Chinese Flap Jacks, 105
Chinese Hot Mustard, 23
Chinese Noodles, 25
Chinese Sausage, 27
Chinese Sausage Grill, 97
Chinese Sausage & Vegetables
  in Filo, 104
Chopping, 13, 14
Cilantro, 10, 20
Clams with Spicy Brown Bean
  Sauce, 55
Classical Creations, 126 - 156
Classic Chinese Fried Rice, 48
Classic Stir Fry Sauce, 10, 21
Classic Stir Fry Sauce, Steak
  with, 65
Classic Sweet & Sour Pork, 98
Cleaver, Chinese, 10, 12
Corn, Baby, 20
Corn & Crab Soup, Creamy, 49
Cornstarch, 21
Creamy Corn & Crab Soup, 49
Crescent Moons, 85
Critic's Choice, 146
Crushing, 14
Culinary Regions of China, 7
Curried Chicken
  Dumplings, 129
Curried Chicken & Tofu, 53
Curry, 21

Curry-flavored Deviled Eggs, 40

D
Daikon, 21
Deep-fried Seafood &
  Vegetables, 87
Deep-frying, 17
Deep-frying & Red-cooking, 17
Deluxe Fried Rice, 74
Dicing & Cubing, 14, 15
Dragon's Broth, 103
Dried Black Mushrooms, 10, 23

E
East-West Omelet, 76
East-West Salad, 80
Eggplant, Chinese, 10, 22
Eggs, Curry-flavored Deviled, 40
Eight Treasures, 156
Emerald Bonsai, 44
Emperor's Good Fortune, 61
Emperor's Secret, 152
Empress-style Pears, 100

F
Family Fare, 68
Family-style Meat &
  Vegetables, 95
Fermented Tea, 35, 36
Fiery Roots of Spring, 42
Filo, Chinese Sausage &
  Vegetables in, 104
Fish Fillet Olé, 57
Fish Fillets, Salsa-topped, 57
Fish Fillet with Spicy Brown
  Bean Sauce, 56
Fish, Oriental Steamed
  Whole, 113
Five-spice Chicken
  Drummets, 84
Five-Spice, Chinese, 22
Flank Steak, Three Pepper, 63
Flash Cooking, 19
Flower Drums, 84
Foil-wrapped Chicken, 127
Fowl For All Seasons, 60
Fresh Ginger, 10, 22
Fresh Vegetables with
  Spicy Dip, 39

Fried Rice, Classic Chinese, 48
Fried Rice, Deluxe, 74
From The Garden, 111
Fruit Salad with Sweet &
  Sour Dressing, 69

G
Garden Dynasty, 39
Gelatin, Almond-Coconut, 153
Ginger, Candied, 22
Ginger, Fresh, 10, 22
Glazed Pork Spareribs, 137
Gold Velvet, 49
Golden Phoenix, 143
Golden Triangles, 71
Green Onion Pancakes, 105
Green Tea, 35, 36
Grilled Bacon & Chicken
  Kebabs, 112
Grilled Pork Sausage &
  Vegetables, 97
Guangzhou Scallops, 88

H
Heavenly Cloud, 153
Hoisin Sauce, 10, 23
Homemade Fortune
  Cookies, 124
Hot Mustard, Chinese 23
Hot & Sour Soup, 103

I
Imperial Peking Duck, 141
Individual Lemon Custard
  Tarts, 154
Indonesian Chicken Soup, 134
Indonesian Turnovers, 129
Instant Impressions, 38 - 69

K
Kebabs, Grilled Bacon &
  Chicken, 112
Korean Donburi, 81
Korean Fire & Ice, 135
Korean Teriyaki Sauce, 10, 23
Kung Pao Shrimp, 89

L
Lamb Stew, Braised, 138

Lamb & Vegetable Stir-fry, 120
Laughing Clams, 55
Lemon Chicken, 82
Lemon Custard Tarts,
  Individual, 154
Lettuce-wrapped Turkey &
  Vegetables, 52
Lobster David, 149
Long Grain Rice, 26
Lychee, 10, 23

M
Make A Fortune, 124
Mandarin Marinade, 10, 24
Mandarin Pancakes, 140
Mandarin-style Meat
  Dumplings, 106
Mandarin Treasure, 50
Matchstick, 14, 15
Meat Dumplings,
  Mandarin-style, 106
Medium Grain Rice, 26
Meat & Vegetables,
  Family-style, 95
Minced Pork, Spicy
  Noodles with, 79
Mincing, 14
Ming Coins 72
Mixed Media, 69
Mongolian Fire Pot, 95
Mongolian Lamb, 120
Mushroom Caps, Veal-filled, 72
Mushrooms, Braised Straw,
  Button & Black, 111
Mushrooms, Dried Black, 10, 24
Mushrooms, Straw, 24
Mu Shu Pork, 119

N
Naked Noodles, 77
Nesting Chicken, 142
Noodles, Bean Thread, 10, 24
Noodles, Chinese, 25
Noodles, Rice Stick, 25
Noodles, Seafood with
  Pan-fried, 114

O
Oil, Chili, 20

Oranges, Sweet & Sour
  Chicken with, 50
Oriental Bacon Burgers, 92
Oriental Beverages, 36
Oriental Pantry, 20 - 31
Oriental Steamed Whole
  Fish, 113
Oriental Vegetables,
  Scallops with, 88
Osyter Sauce, Broccoli with, 44
Oven-baked Short Ribs, 116
Oxtail & Daikon Casserole, 139
Oyster Sauce, 25

P
Pagoda Pork Chops, 96
Pancakes, Thin Chinese, 140
Pancakes with Stir-fried Pork &
  Vegetables, 119
Pears with Candied Ginger
  Sauce, 100
Peking Chicken Skewers, 112
Peking Duck, 141
Plan Your Own Menu, 32
Plum Sauce, 25
Pork Buns, Steamed, 128
Pork, Chinese Barbecued, 136
Pork Chops with Onion,
  Spicy, 96
Pork, Classic Sweet & Sour, 98
Pork Dumplings in Broth, 133
Pork Dumplings, Steamed, 131
Pork Sausage & Vegetables,
  Grilled, 97
Pork Spareribs, Glazed, 137
Pork & Summer Vegetables, 68
Pork & Vegetables, Pancakes
  with Stir-fried, 119
Potato Salad, Chili-flavored, 73
Potstickers, 106
Preserved Vegetables,
  Szechuan, 26

R
Rainbow Fruit Medley, 101
Red-cooked Lamb, 138
Red-cooking, 18
Repeat Performance, 139

Ribs, Braised Orange-
  flavored, 117
Rice-filled Whole Chicken, 143
Rice In A Rush, 48
Rice, Long Grain, 26
Rice, Medium Grain, 26
Rice, Short Grain, 26
Rice Pudding, Sweet, 156
Rice Salad, Turkey, 61
Rice Stick Noodles, 25
Rice To The Occasion, 74
Rice, Vegetarian Curried, 108
Rice Vinegar, 30
Rice Wine, 30
Roll Cutting, 14, 15

S
Salmon Steaks, Teriyaki, 58
Salmon Steaks, Wok-
  smoked, 152
Salsa-topped Fish Fillets, 57
Sanjook, 66
Sausage, Chinese, 27
Savory Chicken Wings, 109
Savory Sensations, 102 - 125
Scallops with Oriental
  Vegetables, 88
Scarlet Warrior, 90
Scented Tea, 35, 37
Seafood & Vegetables,
  Deep-fried, 87
Seafood with Pan-fried
  Noodles, 114
Seasonal Harvest, 45
Seoul Bones, 116
Semi-fermented Tea, 35, 36
Sesame-coated Cream
  Cheese Appetizers, 41
Sesame Cookies, 125
Sesame Noodles, 77
Sesame Oil, 27
Short Grain Rice, 26
Short Ribs, Oven-baked, 116
Shredding, 14, 15
Shrimp & Chicken Soup with
  Rice Crusts, 132
Shrimp Toast, 71
Shrimp with Four Flavors, 89

Silver Noodles, Chili-flavored
  Crab with, 90
Singapore Sins, 40
Sisters From The Sea, 114
Siu Mai, 131
Sizzling Rice Soup, 132
Skewered Beef & Green
  Onions, 66
Slice & Dice, 13
Slicing, 13, 14
Sorbets, Assorted Fruit, 122
Soto Ayam, 134
Soup, Creamy Corn & Crab, 49
Soup, Hot & Sour, 103
Soup, Shrimp & Chicken with
  Rice Crusts, 132
Soy Sauce, 27
South China Sea Catch, 56
Spicy Asparagus Appetizer, 42
Spicy Brown Bean Sauce, 10, 28
Spicy Brown Bean Sauce,
  Clams with, 55
Spicy Brown Bean Sauce,
  Fish Fillet with, 56
Spicy Chicken & Vegetables, 47
Spicy Korean Chicken Salad, 135
Spicy Noodles with Minced
  Pork, 79
Spicy Pork Chops with
  Onion, 96
Spicy Spuds, 73
Star Anise, 28
Steak Oriental, 65
Steak with Classic Stir Fry
  Sauce, 65
Steamed Pork Buns, 128
Steamed Pork Dumplings, 131
Steamers, 10, 12
Steaming, 19
Steaming & Flash Cooking, 19
Stir, Braise & Glaze, 16
Stir-fried Chicken Teriyaki
  over Rice, 81
Stir-fried Pork & Vegetables,
  Pancakes with, 119
Stir-fried Seasonal
  Vegetables, 45
Stir-frying, 16
Straw Mushrooms, 24

Sweet Red Bean Paste, 28
Sweet Rice Pudding, 156
Sweet & Sour Chicken with
  Oranges, 50
Sweet & Sour Dressing, Fruit
  Salad with, 69
Sweet & Sour Pork, 98
Sweet & Sour Stir Fry
  Sauce, 10, 28
Sweet & Sour Veal in
  Peppers, 121
Szechuan Fowl Play, 47
Szechuan Noodle Toss, 79
Szechuan Peppercorns, 28
Szechuan Preserved
  Vegetables, 26
Szechuan Spicy Stir Fry
  Sauce, 10, 29

T
Tangy Bird, 82
Tea, 36
Tea, Fermented, 35, 36
Tea, Green, 35, 36
Tea, Scented, 35, 36
Tea, Semi-fermented, 35, 36
Tea-smoked Chicken, 146
Teriyaki Turkey, Stir-fry, 60
Teriyaki Salmon Steaks, 58
Thin Chinese Pancakes, 140
Three Pepper Flank Steak, 63
Tiger Lily Buds, 29
Timely Temptations, 70 - 101
Time-to-spare Ribs, 117
Tofu, 29
Toishan Veal, 121
Tomato Beef, 64
Tools For Good Cooking, 8
Tropical Ices, 122
Trout with Seafood Stuffing,
  Braised, 151
Tsang Spring Rolls, 104
Tsang Tarts, 154
Tsang Tempura, 87
Turkey Bundles, 52
Turkey Rice Salad, 61
Turkey Teriyaki Stir-fry, 60
Turkey & Vegetables, Lettuce-
  wrapped, 52

V
Veal-filled Mushroom Caps, 72
Veal in Peppers, Sweet &
  Sour, 121
Vegetable Omelet, 76
Vegetables, Fresh with
  Spicy Dip, 39
Vegetables, Stir-fried
  Seasonal, 45
Vegetarian Curried Rice, 108
Vinegar, Rice, 30

W
Water Chestnuts, 10, 30
Wine, 35, 37
Wine, Rice, 30, 35
Wok, 8, 10
Wok Oil, 10, 30
Wok-smoked Salmon Steaks, 152
Won Ton Soup, 133
Wood Ears, 10, 30
Wrappers, 31

Y
Yellow Sea Dragon, 113